A
PLACE
CALLED
THERE

KINGSLEY FLETCHER

A PLACE CALLED THERE

Where Contentment and Desire Meet

Treasure House
An Imprint of

Destiny Image® Publishers, Inc.
P.O. Box 310
Shippensburg, PA 17257-0310

"For where your treasure is, there will your heart be also."
Matthew 6:21

ISBN 0-7684-3018-6

For Worldwide Distribution
Printed in the U.S.A.

This book and all other Destiny Image, Revival Press, MercyPlace, Fresh Bread, Destiny Image Fiction, and Treasure House books are available at Christian bookstores and distributors worldwide.

2 3 4 5 6 7 8 9 10 / 09 08 07 06 05 04 03

For a U.S. bookstore nearest you, call
1-800-722-6774.
For more information on foreign distributors, call
717-532-3040.
Or reach us on the Internet:
www.destinyimage.com

DEDICATION

I Dedicate This Book to…

…all those who believe in the all-present moving God, the God of sequence and God of transition—those who are strategically but deliberately taking steps from where they are to realms they've never been.

…to those who have been hungry, seeking and knocking; those who don't know where to turn—those who desire to fulfill the quest to seek deeper things in God. This book is meant to reach you and all those who have come through real threats, struggles, met disappointments and disillusionment yet have stood their ground—believing by faith that God will bring them through.

…to those forty-four heads of state who, in spite of their political and economic successes, still know that there is "*A Place Called There*" and have given me the honor and pleasure of mentoring them to this special place.

…to the many social, political, business and religious leaders around the world with whom I have been blessed to forge a common purpose through fellowship to explore "*A Place Called There.*"

…to all of you holding this book in your hands right now—those of you committed to taking a journey to a place you've never been—to "*A Place Called There!*" May God richly bless you as you make this pilgrimage with Him!

ACKNOWLEDGEMENTS

First and foremost I wish to acknowledge our Lord Jesus Christ who, through His grace and mercy, has allowed me the honor and privilege to receive His faithful guidance and help in this journey to *"A Place Called There."*

I want to acknowledge my precious family—my wonderful wife, companion, friend, partner in ministry and the love of my life, Martha Fletcher; along with my special thanks to our lovely daughters, Anna-Kissel and Damaris Joy. Their constant love and willing understanding as I travel the nations of the world enables me to continue fulfilling the purpose and destiny God has ordained for my life.

Also, I want to acknowledge my able and trusted assistant, Paula Diley, who has worked with me for many, many years to ensure the success of all my book projects, and whose tremendous support has meant so very much to me.

I acknowledge the staff of Kingsley Fletcher Ministries and Life Community Church, in appreciation for their dedication to the vision God gave me and for allowing me to speak into their lives on a daily basis.

And last, but not least, I acknowledge all the wonderful Partners and Friends of Kingsley Fletcher Ministries whose love, prayers and support sustain me and allow the ministry to steadily progress. May God richly bless all of you!

TABLE OF CONTENTS

Dedication

Acknowledgments

Chapter One

"WHERE ARE YOU, GOD?"

THROUGHOUT the ages, great men and women of faith have spoken about secret "places" in God. Sadly, many believers do not enter into this place. Many of us do not even know it exists, or that we can enter into it.

In this place in God we can experience Divine favor. This does not mean we will never experience hardship, pain, or sometimes loss. But in this place we will experience a deeper and higher dimension of life—and also a very rare kind of joy to which nothing in the world can compare.

Sadly, to our present world's thinking and also to the inexperienced believer, this place in God remains elusive. A secret. How do I know this is true?

As I travel extensively across the world and share the message of God's love and healing, I hear the same sense of loss and confusion from people in all walks of life. Regardless of one's status economically or socially, there is this deep need for

> *It is the Heavenly Father's will that we should be with Him, in the place where He is.*

fulfillment. One may not necessarily recognize that this is a spiritual void, but they long for a sense of complete fulfillment. So many have the sense that God is secretive, hidden, distant. That we are *here*, on this side of the veil. And God is *there*, not involved in our everyday lives at all. We struggle, or we feel flat or directionless, and we wonder, "Where are you, God? Do you hear me? Why am I here and what is my purpose in life?"

Is God playing hide-and-seek with me? If He is not, why is there a gap between us? God does not want this sense of distance, this gap, to exist. As Jesus told us, it is the Heavenly Father's will that we should be with Him, in the place where He is.

> *And if I go and prepare a place for you, I will come back and take you to be with me that you also may be where I am.*
> —John 14:3

In this book, we will explore the ways God calls us and helps us to enter into the place where, more and more, we may come to know Him and His holy presence. The place where we will grow to be more and more at one with Him.

God's plan is not content to leave us alone, powerless, and confused here. God wants us to enter into a new place in Him—*a place called there.*

Paul Knew of This Place

The Apostle Paul spoke about his own longing to enter this place in God in this way:

I want to know Christ and the power of His resurrection and the fellowship of sharing in His sufferings, becoming like Him in His death, and so, somehow, to attain to the resurrection from the dead.

—Philippians 3:10-11

Paul uses the most powerful, and even disturbing, words to make his point. He speaks about going through things that are most unpleasant. Suffering. Death. And he speaks of coming out on the other side in a new place. A place where we experience a whole new kind of life.

Here is Paul—the great apostle who went through so much *before* coming to Christ, and even more *after* coming to Christ. You would think he had "arrived" spiritually, wouldn't you? But he knew there is always more to be attained in God. Paul is saying, "Yes, I am saved and filled with God's Spirit. Yes, I know God has promised me great things. But I also know there is a place in God that is the very source of a new kind of life—a manifestation of God's presence and power so strong it can raise the dead. If only I can know this place in God, where there is this kind of power." That is a very compelling statement.

What this passage tells me is this: *As good a relationship as Paul had with God, he knew there was a deeper place in the Spirit.* And he was not going to be satisfied until he pressed on, and pressed into it.

We would do well to pause and grasp the importance of this powerful statement from Paul.

KNOWING ABOUT GOD, AND EVEN KNOWING GOD... IS NOT THE SAME AS ENTERING IN

Some of you reading this book may know all about God. That is, you've heard that there is a God and believe He exists. What you need is to begin the spiritual journey in God by opening your heart and mind to receive the fullness of His Son, Jesus Christ.

Others of you have been believers for some time. You've followed Him and known Him. And yet you find yourself so often in the same place many unbelievers find themselves. If you are honest, you feel powerless in your life. Your life seems without purpose or direction. Or perhaps it's not that way at all. In your walk with God you have seen your own prayers answered. Occasionally, you even experienced miracles and unexplainable acts of God. But still *something* is missing.

> *Many of us want just enough of God to make our troubles go away.*

If that's so, you are in good company.

Paul knew God in a way that few of us know Him. From his earliest days his desire to know God was intense—so intense, in fact, it gave him a zeal to persecute the Church when he believed those who were followers after Jesus Christ were blaspheming God by worshipping Jesus. In his blind desperation to serve God, he persecuted them with passion.

Even Paul, the great miracle-working apostle, knew there was a place in God he had not reached.

And when Paul discovered the truth—that Jesus is God in the flesh—he threw himself into serving Him. He considered everything else to be of no importance except for knowing the One he loved the most, that is, Christ Jesus. And what experiences Paul had! Imagine being so saturated with the power of God that he could speak to a man who was trying to pervert the way of the Lord—"You will be blind for a season" (Acts 13:11)—and instantly God went to work on Paul's behalf and took the man's sight. Yet this great apostle of God said, "What I know of God is not enough!"

Paul realized there is a place in God that he had not reached. He had given the best of his knowledge, but he still wanted to know and experience more. He realized that knowing about God, and even knowing God in great measure, is not the same thing as entering into the depths of God—which is the only place where we can experience the true source of limitless life and joy.

MANY ARE CALLED

"I'm not satisfied with my life," a man said to me recently, "and I don't understand it. I have a good family, a good home, a good job. What is wrong with me?"

This man, an unbeliever, is not so different from the believers who frequently tell me similar things. "Dr. Fletcher," a believer told me, "I had a dramatic conversion, and I've experienced answers to prayer. But my spiritual life is lacking something." A woman said to me, "In the past two years I've witnessed great moves of God. Why am I so spiritually dry?"

In fact, a minister of the gospel, a wonderful man of God, recently confided to me: "I have been a believer for decades. I followed God, served Him and His people as faithfully as I know how.

I've been as true to my calling as I know how to be. But I feel almost empty inside."

Each of these persons, and many more like them, speak of a discontent. They are all looking, perhaps without even knowing it, for *something*.

When we are discontent in our spirit, what we need is to hear the voice and the Word of God. We need to have our souls stirred, and to be awakened by the same voice that spoke to Paul so dramatically he actually fell off his horse (see Acts 9:1-7). This turning-point in Paul's life occurred after Jesus' death and burial—but the Jesus who spoke to Paul was most definitely not dead! He said to Paul, in effect, "Let me tell you something, you are hearing a voice that is not in the grave. You are listening to the voice of the Resurrected One."

Paul heard the voice—from God himself—and recognized it as the voice of the Ever-Living One. Many of us, believer and unbeliever alike, have also heard God calling to us. We hear it in the stirring discontent that troubles our souls. As Scripture tells us: *"Many are called but few are chosen"* (Matthew 22:14).

You see, there is a difference between Paul and many of us. When we realize we are discontent, and we turn to God, we usually want just enough of God to make the troubling feelings go away. What we want is for God to make us feel good, comfortable, maybe even "spiritual." *We want our needs and our wants to be satisfied.* But that is where we draw the line.

Paul was different. Yes, he would suffer discouragements, setbacks, troubles, temptations, and trials, just like us. After the voice of God called him, all of Paul's energy—his passion, his motivation—was turned around and used for one thing only: *to conform to the will of God.* Paul wanted to go all the way for God.

What did Paul find as he pressed deeper and deeper into the Father? He tells us over and over again in his letters to the Church: *"I will come to you with joy"* (Romans 15:32); *"I am full of joy"* (Romans 16:19); *"[I] work with you for your joy"* (2 Corinthians 1:24); *"My joy is greater than ever"* (2 Corinthians 7:7). Joy was one of the chief signs that he, and other believers, were pressing into God. Joy was so

> *Even Paul, the great miracle-working apostle, knew there was a place in God he had not reached.*

much a measure of their place in God that when the Galatians fell from grace back into the law Paul asked, *"What has happened to all your joy?"* (Galatians 4:15).

But is that *really* what most of us want—to press into *God?* All my experience as a pastor and minister of Christ have shown me that the answer is *no.* We want God...but we want Him for what He can do for us. We want God for *our* sake. All our desiring brings us right back to where we began—that is, back to our very little selves.

It is very sad, really. Even the best of us—when we were not committed to God—were once committed to the devil full-time. Now, those of us who are believers have changed our employer. We received a pink slip from the devil and God is now our full-time employer. It is very sad, however, that for all the devotion and commitment we gave to the devil we now give only *one-tenth* of it to the Lord! Some of us used to dance the night away. Now that we have come to Christ we don't use the same strength to dance for Him. We

> *"More of God" doesn't come when we have committed ourselves to giving the least amount possible.*

used to spend all our life-savings on the devil. Now that we have been saved, many of us say, "I have to be wise and prudent with my money. We then withhold all but the ten percent." At the same time we say, "God, something is wrong inside. I want more of you."

"More of God" doesn't come when we have committed ourselves to giving the least amount possible. God is wiser. He says, *"Give and it shall be given to you"* (Luke 6:38).

If we want to find that place in God where life and joy come from, we must, like Paul, prove that we will meet God at least halfway. If we meet Him even halfway He will take us *all* the way.

ALL THE WAY "THERE"

Sometimes people approach me with a puzzled look and say, "I notice that you often speak to unbelievers in your messages the same way you speak to believers. Why is that?"

I answer them, "Because both believers and unbelievers can suffer from the same problem."

"What is that?" they ask.

My reply: "*Unbelief.*"

Now it certainly is true that every believer has a measure of belief in God. By that, I do not mean a mere head knowledge of God. I mean an honest, heart-knowledge of God which comes from personal encounter. Most of us know God and have some kind of knowledge and experience with God because we have been in His presence. At times, He has graciously visited with us, and at other times we have sought Him. Being in His presence has left its mark upon us. We have carried away a sweet scent of Him, a deep-soul memory that clings to us and reminds us of His goodness. In those few moments with Him we may whisper, or even shout, "You are God! All-powerful and ever-living. There is nothing you cannot do!"

Then, however, we return to our everyday lives and quickly forget Him and what He is like. We encounter conflicts at work, struggles in our families. We experience threats to our health or finances. We run into people whose hearts are hard toward us and cold toward God. We may even experience a more serious crisis and face the prospect of death. Then all of our spiritual feeling drains out of us, and we're right back to what Paul calls "the old man" or "the old self.

> *For we know that our old self was crucified with him so that the body of sin might be rendered powerless, that we should no longer be slaves to sin.*
>
> —Romans 6:6

That is also to say—that we should no longer be subjected to a worldly, faithless way of thinking. We're right back to living in unbelief.

Now don't get me wrong. I love being in the presence of God. I love to sense God when He is on His throne, and to worship Him while I am there. But the purpose of being in God's presence is to receive something we will need to put to work when we are not in

His presence. We need enough revelation of His majesty to create in us an increasing measure of confidence in Him.

I am speaking of the times in life when God seems to remove himself from us. When circumstances cloud our vision and our hearts are shaken or cold and dead. If we have confidence in God, we will seek Him when He no longer seems to be on the throne. When the throne of God seems vacant and chaos or suffering or evil seem to be reigning, that is when we need to use our confidence in God to seek Him *behind the throne.*

Unfortunately, those are the times in our lives when we are most likely to listen to the voices of the world, the flesh, and the devil, telling us, "Do you see? It was a mistake to follow God. He has left you on your own." Many of us give in. We quit, and don't go all the way.

These are the times, however, when we must go around behind the throne of God. When we must go past the praise by which we enter His courts, and beyond the worship by which we dwell in His magnificent and inspiring presence...and seek Him *in His secret chambers.* When our anxiety, fear, depression, despair drive us to seek God farther than we have been before...then we begin to find Him in His fullness.

This is when the deeper, more powerful, more joyful Christian life really begins. Because the fullness of God is our source of enduring life...and only the fullness of God will take us all the way there.

SEEKING GOD'S FULLNESS

Paul was no stranger to hardship. Listen to him recount his struggles.

I have been in prison many times...flogged severely...exposed to death....Five times I received the forty lashes minus one....Three times I was beaten with rods, once I was stoned, three times I was shipwrecked. I have been constantly on the move. I have been in danger from rivers...from bandits...and from my own countrymen.... I have labored and toiled and often gone without sleep. I have known hunger and thirst and gone without food. I have been cold and naked. And besides everything else, I face the daily pressure of my own concern for all the churches.

—2 Corinthians 11:23-28

> *When our anxiety, fear, depression, despair drive us to seek God farther than we have been before...then we begin to find Him in His fullness.*

Perhaps most painful of all, Paul tells us,

I was [also] given a thorn in the flesh, a messenger of Satan, to torment me...[and] I pleaded with the Lord to take it away from me.

—2 Corinthians 12:7-8

In all his terrible struggles, Paul must surely have heard the voices inside, telling him to give up and turn back from following God. But Paul was not like many of us. He held on to the confidence in God he had gained while spending hours in prayer and worship at the throne of God. In his toughest times, Paul became even more determined. He set His course—not for the throne of God, but for the secret chamber behind the throne. And he said, *"I press on!"* (Philippians 3:14)

Paul entered the secret chambers of God and was stunned by God's deeper revelation of the fullness of God. Paul reports that in this place he was in ecstasy (2 Corinthians 12:2-6)—which is nothing other than sheer and unspeakable *joy*!

No wonder he was empowered by something from within that few of us discover!

What was it that Paul discovered? And how may we find it?

A DIFFERENT KIND OF LIFE

Paul had learned to set his course for that secret place in God. At the same time he knew that, in order to reach this place, an old way of living had to die.

Why? Because Paul understood that there is a *different kind of life* available to us when we enter into the fullness of God. Paul was caught up to the third heaven and saw and heard *"inexpressible things that a man is not permitted to tell"* (2 Corinthians 12:4). He was so overwhelmed by what he saw that forever after he was marked deep within his innermost being. What he experienced in the secret chamber of God gave him the power to overcome everything—and with *joy*!

From that day on, he continually longed to experience the kind of life that he had touched while he was caught up in the presence of the Lord. He hungered and thirsted for it, because, as he wrote,

...if that same Spirit that raised Jesus from the dead is in you, it will quicken your mortal bodies.

—Romans 8:11

The Bible clearly states that our mortal bodies are only temporary. There is a better, resurrected body which we shall receive. Paul was not speaking against the physical body, nor did he have some kind of sick death-wish as he longed for this other kind of life. He was telling us, however, "Though you can't experience immortality right now—not fully, at any rate—your body will eventually weaken and die. But, you *can* experience the same Spirit, anointing, and freshness of life-giving power that raised Jesus from death to immortality. You can experience it in such a way that your own mortal body will affirm that God is the God of all life. God of the living and the dead! He is almighty beyond our wildest imaginations and there is nothing impossible for Him!"

Here we are, right back at the point of our little bit of faith. The reason we conclude there are things God cannot do...the reason our belief contains so much unbelief...is because we have never experienced this kind of powerful life flowing into us. We have not experienced *resurrection life.*

This is not to say we have never experienced some bit of God's power. For some who are reading this book, experiencing the power to get beyond your discouragement and doubt enough to look for God at all has required the power of God working in you. God always seeks, calls, and empowers us for the work. Some have experienced receiving the power to speak in tongues, to study and understand the deep things of Scripture, or to prophesy, witness, or preach.

But what we need, what our souls long for, are the depths.

YOU MAY BE *LONGING*...BUT ARE YOU ALSO *WILLING*?

You and I need the resurrection power of God. We need it to produce in our very flesh the witness of the power of the resurrection. We need it so that we do not stay stuck in the beginning stages of faith, where we only seek God for our own comfort. We need the resurrection power of God because we will face hardship and suffering, emptiness and longing, desire for meaning and purpose. We need it to produce works of righteousness and faith, so that our lives will not be wasted on useless and vain pastimes.

> *What he experienced in the secret chamber of God gave him the power to overcome everything—and with joy!*

What holds you back from seeking God in the fullness of His power?

We can find this place in God—the secret place...*there, where we too may encounter the power of resurrection life!* God is more than willing, He is yearning for you to meet Him there.

If we want to find it, however, it will cost us something. It will cost us the very things we know are of no benefit to us in our relationship with God. It will cost us our pursuits, our dreams and ambitions, the security we seek in possessions and position. It will cost us relationships that are ungodly.

What are the things in your life that are holding you back from seeking God in His fullness? And what value are they, in comparison to knowing His powerful resurrection life in your very being?

In the chapters that follow we will see how to find that place in God—in our seeking, in prayer, in darkness, in serving, and in God himself. We will allow God's Word to tell us what it is to dwell with Him in the mighty power of His Spirit.

> *What holds you back from seeking God in the fullness of His power?*

For now, we will let Paul have the final say, sending us on our way with a prayer he offers on behalf of all who seek God, and the fullness of deeper life in Him. Paul says:

> *...I kneel before the Father, from whom His whole family in heaven and on earth derives its name. I pray that out of His glorious riches He may strengthen you with power through His Spirit in your inner being, so that Christ may dwell in your hearts through faith. And I pray that you, being rooted and established in love, may have power, together with all the saints, to grasp how wide and long and high and deep is the love of Christ, and to know this love that surpasses knowledge—that you may be filled to the measure of all the fullness of God.*
>
> —Ephesians 3: 14-19

You see, Paul asks God to give us the very thing for which our hearts are truly yearning. To be caught up in the deep love of God, filled to "all fullness and overflowing"—with the graceful and life-giving love of God.

May you recognize this as your desire. May you pursue it with all your heart, until nothing else matters so much. And may you press in, until you find what your heart is hungering for!

And now we will turn to the place where our journey begins...and that is, the place of seeking.

Chapter Two

_____

A PLACE...IN SEEKING

_____

As in all ages, people today are seeking. We want to find the place where we can finally rest and stop seeking. We want a place of ultimate contentment and happiness.

Many of us are seeking that place by trying to create security for ourselves in this world. Some of us want nice things. A good house, a great job, a devoted spouse, well-behaved children, caring friends.

Some are struggling at a more basic level, just to have any place, anyone, or anything to hold onto and call their own. Many are utterly stressed-out by all their seeking and striving, and what they think they want most is just peace and quiet.

Many believers, likewise, are dissatisfied and seeking. They are confused because they thought that when they gave their lives to the Lord and accepted His free gift of salvation their search was over. But inside they are restless and discontent.

Some other believers I know are content—but not with a true satisfaction. They're content to stay right where they are in their faith. They've gotten a little bit of blessing. A little bit of security. A little bit of friendship from their church family. "This is good enough, Lord," they think. "Just keep my life exactly the way it is now and I'll be fine, thank you." Inwardly, however, they are not really satisfied. One day, when a strong cold wind shakes the foundations of their life they will realize they have stopped to make their camp at an earthly oasis...which will turn out to be an illusion. How quickly and how easily the securities and satisfactions of this world vanish.

> *God is no fool. He keeps within Himself the one thing we are all looking for— "fullness of joy."*

What confuses believers, I think, is that most of us were taught that our top priority is to "sit at Jesus feet." Perhaps we've heard the story of Jesus' visit with Mary and Martha (see Luke 10). Martha busied herself, while Mary sat at Jesus' feet, listening, delighting in His presence. When Martha rebuked Mary, Jesus stopped her. *"She has chosen what is better"* (v. 42). Please notice Jesus did not say, "She has chosen what is best."

Many of us believe that "sitting at Jesus' feet"—which winds up meaning, sitting contentedly in the church pew—is the best thing we can have or do. It's odd we think this way, when the Bible clearly describes the Christian life, not as a "sit" but as a "walk." Many people, unbeliever and believer alike, are sitting here in the midst of our lives, and inside we feel stuck. Is it any wonder that, as a whole culture, we are so unhappy? Is it any wonder that, every year, companies that sell prescription drugs for depression break their previous sales records?

If you are feeling stuck—whether in bland self-satisfaction or in dismal depression—it is time to hear the voice of God calling to you again. He is not sitting still. He is always moving on ahead of us, He wants us to be with Him *"where He is"* (John 14:3). And so His is the voice inside, asking, "Where can I find the life of joy and deep satisfaction?"

Isn't that what you are saying: "God, I want more?"

You must be willing to set out again, from where you are stopped or stuck, and begin to seek God again.

WHAT WE'RE ALL SEEKING

The good news is that we are never alone in our seeking. Jesus promised to take us to be, "with God, where He is." Why? Because that is the most wonderful place to be. You see, God is no fool. He keeps within himself the one thing we are all looking for— *"fullness of joy"* (Psalm 16:11). And along the way, He gives us the Holy Spirit to be our friend and guide (see John 16:13).

At the same time, God is not miserly with us, His children. He does not withhold joy from us until and unless we make our way fully to Him. All along the way, throughout our lives, He treats us to lesser joys—giving us good things to delight us. How many of us really make use of all the joy the Lord gives us? We are really like little children when it comes to spiritual matters.

Many of us seem to find our "delight" in walking around with long faces. Some take delight in being unhappy, mean, cynical, or depressed. Why? Because that is probably how we get attention, or get our way. How foolish, to be miserable all the time to get other people to give you what you want. Whether that is the case with you or not, I know people who never smile, and their faces are so dry that if they were even to grin, their face would crack. This is as true of many Christians as it is unbelievers.

I used to think that being a spiritual person, holy and devout, meant that you had to have a serious demeanor. I thought that being sober-faced was the look of holiness. That's what many of us are taught. Then we wonder why people are not drawn to us. Our faces look tight, unhappy, sometimes even mean. People think, "Man, he looks too serious." Or, "If she is a believer in God, why is she so unhappy?" They are scared to come to us, or they think our religion is a failure.

Despite all our foolishness, God is a good Father. He does what any earthly parent does when He sees his children are miserable. He tries to get them to feel joy. He wants us to share in the joy that radiates from the fullness that is in Him. To begin with, He wants to get us to crack a smile! If only He can get us to sense that we will not find life in our unhappiness and manipulations, but in seeking joy!

Imagine God having you as His child. He walks with you by His Spirit, and He watches to see where you are unhappy or miserable. Like any parent, He knows there is a way to get small children to laugh. All you've got to do is just play with them. This is even true with babies. You smile, you wiggle your fingers… and I don't care how unhappy the baby looks, he will soon smile.

"I am a very happy man," one successful businessman told me recently. "I have power. I have success. I have everything I ever dreamed of." A woman also said to me, "I have my children. I have a career. I have a happy life." The cloud behind their eyes told a different truth.

A very intensely-devout, Christian lady came up to me recently. Everything she said was prefaced by, "The Lord told me this" or "The Lord wants me to do that." But in her eyes—no delight!

You may be thinking, "But I'm not unhappy. I'm not down."

What does your face say? You see, your face is a reflection of what is happening in your spirit.

If you are still objecting, if you think that smiling and laughter is not a sign of spiritual health, then you need to read your Bible. The scriptures tell us that God sits in heaven, and out of His deep joy, He laughs (see Psalm 2:4).

When you see any "saved, sanctified, spiritual" believer who never laughs, you are around a mean, sanctified machine. If a believer doesn't have real joy, I know that when I'm hurting that person can't help me. I do not mean that we should laugh-off, or make light of pain, but true joy is like a spiritual medicine. If you don't have any medicine, I will not bring my sickness to you because your treatment may kill me. I look for people whose faces, even when they are serious, somehow radiate the life and grace that come from deep deposits of joy. That radiant joy is like medicine for the body and life for the soul.

This is why, whenever you are discontented and begin to seek, it is God you are really after. Whatever else you may think you are seeking, you are in truth looking for a joy that is without end—and there is only one place where you will find that.

> *Your face is a reflection of what is happening in your spirit.*

LOOKING INTO THE HEART OF GOD

Perhaps you have been troubled and sought help or counsel from a spiritual friend. Maybe you have heard the advice, "Seek the face of God." Many people throughout history have wanted to see God's face. In the Bible we read about people who "sought the face of God." Why? Because when you can look into someone's face, you can also see what's in their heart. And the same is true with God. If you see His face, you see His heart. When you are seeking, it helps greatly if you know where your goal is and what you'll find once you are there.

Beginning in Exodus, the Bible gives us a profound revelation. Let me set the stage.

Moses has been restless. We think of him as a great spiritual giant. But his soul was not at ease or satisfied. Then the God who walked with Moses—out of Egypt, through the sea, all the way through the wilderness—this God had something more for Moses:

> *Whatever else you may think you are seeking, you are in truth looking for a joy that is without end.*

Now the Lord said to Moses and the leaders of Israel, *"Come up to the Lord and worship from a distance"* (Exodus 24: 1).

You see, our true seeking always begins with worshiping God. That is how we acknowledge Him as the source of all we need.

Moses alone shall approach the Lord; the others must not come near (v. 2).

With great excitement, Moses came down from the mountain and told the people everything the Lord had said.

Then Moses and Aaron, Nadab and Abihu, and seventy of the elders of Israel, went up and saw the God of Israel (v.9).

What a great picture of the love of God! What the Bible is telling us is this: Every one of us, even those who worship God "from a distance" are allowed to catch amazing glimpses of God. No matter where we are in our seeking, God wants us to come nearer to Him. Then, even if we still feel we are at a distance from God, He begins to reveal His love to us. There is something more.

When Moses and the leaders of Israel looked, the Bible tells,

Under [God's] feet was something like a pavement made of sapphire, clear as the sky itself (v.10).

What they saw was a beautiful glimpse of the glory of God, streaming from the throne like a pavement. This is the highway of God's glory on which Jesus, the King and Lord of all, rises and walks throughout creation. Here He stands firmly above everything that lies under His gaze, and over anything that might try to rise against Him. For as Paul tells us later in the New Testament,

God placed all things under [Jesus'] feet and appointed Him to be over everything.
—Ephesians 1:22

From this place of unshakable authority, Paul says, Jesus stands

far above all rule and authority, power and dominion, and every title that can be given, not only in the present age but in the one to come (v. 21).

When we see God in His glory, we see Jesus. And when we see Jesus, we see that He is far more than a "friend." He is, first and foremost, Lord. You see, we have made Him our friend, but that is not the way friendship works with a king. You don't extend friendship to a king, he extends it to you. Jesus extends us His friendship on the basis of servanthood. As the Apostle John tells us, Jesus says,

"You are my friends if you do what I command."
—John 15:14

If we are not His servants, we cannot call ourselves His friends. If we do not do what He says, we can call Him "Lord" all we want— but it means nothing.

God is so gracious to give us these magnificent revelations of Himself in His Word. He shows us His glory—with the heavens and the earth under His feet. He shows us the beauty and strength in which the Lord Jesus walks above all the kingdoms of this world, those that are visible and those that are invisible. As Paul also tells us, nothing has dominion over Christ, neither death nor life, neither angels nor demons, neither the present nor the future, nor any powers, neither height nor depth, nor anything else in all creation (Romans 8:38,39a).

Because He is all-powerful, nothing can stand in His way when He comes to love, protect, and direct the lives of those who are His own. For as Paul says,

[Nothing] can separate us from the love of God that is in Christ Jesus our Lord (v. 39b).

ARE YOU SEEKING?

If you are seeking, the stirring you sense inside is God. It is His way of calling to you. He is the One stirring your heart. What we are all looking for is that deep contentment that comes when we know nothing can rise against us to harm or destroy our peace and the knowledge that we are loved.

God has shown us the way to this place, for it is in Him. It is in Christ Jesus. We enter into this place in Christ by making Him our Lord. In this position, nothing can rise against us that will destroy us. The principalities and powers that fight against us every day, causing us frustration, confusion, and pain are already defeated. As Paul teaches us, we have ultimate peace because the God of peace shall crush satan under your feet shortly (Romans 16:20).

> *If we do not do what He says, we can call Him "Lord" all we want—but it means nothing.*

How does God crush satan under our feet? Satan is crushed the moment you and I recognize that Christ is Lord over everything—the moment we give Him all authority to rule and reign over our lives, entrusting our care and direction to Him. Then He becomes our Lord, and we become His friends.

Hold on a bit, though. Paul adds one little word to his statement. He says God will crush satan "shortly." *Shortly* is the same term that is used elsewhere in Scripture when Jesus says, "I am coming soon" (Revelation 22:12,20). What does it mean, then, that Satan is under Jesus' feet and we will crush him "shortly?"

> *Satan is crushed the moment you and I recognize that Christ is Lord over everything.*

It means that Jesus both walks with us in Spirit now, and as we walk with Him acknowledging His lordship, we share in the dominion He is now spreading over all creation—and He is coming soon to establish the total lordship in which we will share.

If you recognize in yourself a dissatisfaction, whether you are a believer or not, it all comes down to this: You need to change your mentality about Jesus. You may say, "Yes, I believe Jesus is the Lord." Or even "Jesus is my Lord." But do you really have a regard and respect for Jesus' glory and might? Many people have more regard for Britney Spears or Justin Timberlake than they do for Jesus Christ. People are so awed by celebrities they stalk people like these. Paul said he counted everything else as "dung" compared to Jesus. And he left everything behind in the dust to follow hard after Jesus with all his heart. Just as some people stalk celebrities, Paul was a stalker of Jesus.

WHAT ARE YOU AFTER?

Are you seeking Jesus yet? If you are a believer, are you seeking to be with Him in the place where He is today, following beside Him as He establishes His authority over all things? Jesus is looking for men and women who will follow hard after Him.

What are you after in this life? A little bit of peace? Comfort? Accomplishment? Freedom from the penalty of sin? Or are you willing to say, "Wherever you are leading I will go?" To those who say this—those who are His, ready to serve God with Him—Jesus gives

His friendship and authority. Nothing else but this can fill the longing of our hearts.

God has so graciously shown us His glory, that highway in the Spirit where His Son Jesus walks. He shows us where we may walk right beside Him in spirit. For the desire of the Father is that every eye should see His Son exalted.

When we get this revelation, of His splendor, majesty, and might, all our longing and seeking will change. We will no longer be plagued by vague longings, casting about here and there, seeking this or that to fill our emptiness. We will throw all the energy of our lives into seeking and walking with Him.

Let us return to Moses again, who had seen the brilliant highway of God's glory streaming out from the throne. His experience has one more thing of great importance to show us.

It must have been so tempting for Moses to settle down right there in the wilderness, and to return again and again to the same spot on the mountain where he and the leaders of Israel caught the amazing glimpse of God. In a sense, that is what many of us do. We experience a touch of God—perhaps out in nature, or in church during praise and worship—and we want to settle down right there. We return over and over to our favorite place, our favorite praise choruses, hoping to get that wonderful feeling again. We hope we will find that inner satisfaction we had before.

Yet the satisfaction is gone. No matter how many times we revisit the beautiful place, and no matter how many times we try to excite our spirits again by singing the same songs, the joy is not there. That is because our satisfaction is always and only found in God Himself. There are places and times that usher us into His presence…but when we try to find Him in the same old places we find He has gone.

If we are spiritual thrill-seekers, that is all we will ever find. Thrills that quickly become empty, no matter how "godly" they first appear. To find continual satisfaction we must seek it in God Himself. So we must follow Him closely and move when He moves.

Moses understood this. In Exodus 33 God tells him,

"Leave this place, you and the people you brought up out of Egypt, and go to the land I promised on oath (v. 1).

He also tells Moses,

"I will send an angel before you….But I will not go with you" (v. 2a, 3a).

Moses might have responded the way many of us would. "An angel! That will be thrilling! I can't wait to see what an angel looks like!" Or he might have responded the way many believers would. "This is exactly what I've been seeking, Lord—my life's calling and mission. Sorry you're not coming, Lord, but thanks for giving me a great task to do so I can feel like I have purpose in my life and maybe establish my own glory so people will remember me when I'm gone."

Instead, Moses was grieved. He wanted more than thrills. He wasn't interested in his mission or purpose or personal glory. He replied,

"If I have found favor with you, Lord, teach me your ways, so I may know you and continue to find favor with you" (v. 13).

His heart was hard after God, and he begged the Lord, saying,

"If your presence does not go with us, do not send us up from here" (v. 15).

Teach me your ways. Let me walk with you. Don't send me out to walk alone on my own way. Do not let me live my life, or take on any purpose or mission that is without you. That was the desire of Moses' heart.

In God's reply to Moses, you can almost hear how pleased God is:

"My presence will go with you...and I will give you rest" (v. 14).

A PLACE IN SEEKING

How many of us seek the Lord, only to tell Him, "Lord, this is the way I see it. And this is the way I want to do it. Will you help me?"

You see, we cannot have a relationship with God that is based on our agenda. We want God to walk in our ways, but God follows no one. He leads. We find Him and the satisfaction He gives when we say, "Lord, lead me where you want to go. Show me what it is you want me to accomplish and what you want me to do as I serve you with my life."

> *To find continual satisfaction we must seek it in God himself.*

Moses and the people of Israel would leave the place they were in when that conversation took place. They would have to roll up their tents, leave the familiar wells, pastures, and resting places they

> *If we are going to walk with God we too may be called on to leave behind that which gives us temporary satisfaction.*

knew. If we are going to walk with God we too may be called on to leave behind that which gives us temporary satisfaction. But the things we try to hold onto don't satisfy us for long, do they? Otherwise we would not be restless in our hearts, and seeking deeper satisfaction, would we? Moses and all Israel would move on.

Is this our fate as followers of God? To be constantly letting go of things and saying goodbye to things that satisfy us? To constantly give up that which we find good in order to faithfully follow after God?

God told Moses, "I will give you rest." And then He said, "Let's move out."

Where is that deep rest and satisfaction for the seeker of God? Moses' experience gives us the answer. God told him,

"There is a place near me where you may stand on a rock. When my glory passes by I will put you in a cleft in the rock and cover you with my hand..." (vv. 19,20).

What are you holding onto that is keeping you from following after God? From finding your joy and satisfaction and life in Him? Let it go, and walk in His ways.

When will you let go of your little agenda—your secret plans, wishes, dreams, and desires—that are holding you back from the only lasting satisfaction there is? That is, life in God himself—hidden in His almighty and loving hand.

Today, if you become a seeker after God alone He will indeed show you His glory. That is the only way you will find the place where deep satisfaction comes from.

I promise you, there in that place you will begin to live with joy unspeakable...and life will never be the same.

Chapter Three

A Place...in Prayer

Agentleman came to see me recently, and he was most unhappy. "My prayers are not being answered," he complained. "I feel like God's unwanted stepchild. I don't know if I can trust God anymore, because no matter how urgent my needs are, He just doesn't seem to move on my behalf. Other people seem to get their prayers answered, but when I talk to God He doesn't seem to listen." As we talked, I found that he had made a big assumption—that if he was God's child by rebirth in Christ, then God would do exactly what he asked for when he prayed.

This brother in Christ was not very different from a woman—an unbeliever—who, not long ago, said to me, "Tell me, Dr. Fletcher—how do I get God to answer my prayers? What's the trick?" Her assumption was that there are certain words you can say, or certain things you can do, to get on God's good side and get Him to use His power for you.

> *Moses was a seeker after God.*

Both of these people—a believer and an unbeliever—were having a very similar experience with prayer. They were asking for things, and getting nowhere. And they both assumed that God was being difficult or fickle or uncaring. As the man put it, "It's like I pray and God is saying, 'Who are *you*?'—as if I'm a total stranger."

They reminded me of the men in Scripture who saw Jesus' disciples manifesting power in their prayers (see Acts 19:14-16). They tried to cast out demons, using the same words the disciples used—"Come out, in the name of Jesus of Nazareth"—but the demons only replied, "Jesus, we know. And Paul, we know. But who are *you*?" There was no power in their prayer.

NO POWER IN PRAYER

Many of us have a similar experience in prayer, don't we? Those of us who are believers are even more perplexed than unbelievers. In many ways we seek to please God with our lives—but why is it our name doesn't appear to register with God when miracles are supposed to occur? God seems to act like He doesn't even know who we are.

The truth is, God our Father knows each one of us by name. We are, none of us, strangers to Him. But, just as in life, having influence is not about *how much you know* as it is about *whom you know*. If you need to exert influence, find favor, get things done; and if you can establish that you know someone who has great power to back you, then usually you will get what you need. You have the power to accomplish great things because you have developed an acquaintance and a relationship with someone important.

There is a place in God in prayer in which mighty things are accomplished. Not everyone finds that place. Because of that, there is much frustration in the body of Christ. Many of us have tried various ways to find this place of favor. We do good things: we read the

Bible, we do nice things to serve God. We also avoid doing things to displease God: we don't kill, we don't lie, we don't cheat, we don't commit adultery.

Why, then, does God not do the things that we ask Him to do? Unanswered prayer becomes a wound, and then a fester. Soon our faith is poisoned, and we want to give up trusting or following God altogether. Many of us just throw up our hands and say, "Well, it's a mystery." Others sit and sulk in the pews. We grudgingly continue going to church, giving our offerings. But in our hearts we're thinking, "God, you *owe* me."

Unfortunately, this seems to be the experience of so many today. Is this the way the Christian life is supposed to be? When it comes to this matter of touching the heart of God, are we missing something?

Touching God's Heart in Prayer

In the previous chapter we saw that, just like us, Moses was a seeker. But Moses was different from many of us. While we seek for answers to prayer and for blessings...while we seek for great and small acts to be accomplished...Moses was a seeker *after God.*

In Exodus 33, God promises to give Moses and the people of Israel a land to call their own. Moses might have said, "Thank you, Lord! Praise your name! You have done great things by giving us what just what we needed! You are a great God!"

There was a little test hidden within God's answer to Moses' prayer. For God told Moses He would answer Moses' prayer for a land of plenty and safety for Israel, *"...but I will not go with you"* (v. 3).

Now Moses could have brushed this little piece of God's reply aside. Israel was getting a homeland—that was certainly a sign of great favor from the Lord. If God didn't come along for the journey—well, that was His prerogative, after all He's a deity and they can be fickle. At least we've got territory to call ours.... But Moses was horrified.

> *God is searching hearts today, looking for men and women who will pray, "Lord, show me your glory."*

"If you do not go with us," he said, adamantly, "we are not moving from this place!" (v.15).

Do not miss this important point: God offered to answer Moses' prayer and give them all a great blessing—but He offered Him a blessing that did not include His living presence. And Moses turned that answer down. He said in effect, "I do not want an answer that does not include you. I do not want to be someplace, God, where you are not. If *you* are not in it, I don't want it."

We see that God was pleased with Moses' reply. Why? Because it revealed Moses' heart. God said,

> *"I will do the very thing you have asked, because I am pleased with you and I know you by name."*
> —Exodus 33:17,18

What was the "name" by which Moses had revealed himself? Some of us might be called, "Seeker After My Self and My Own Way." When Moses refused an answer that did not have God in it he revealed his true name—his identity—to be, "Seeker After God and His Way."

Now Moses did add something extraordinary—a request that would take him on to that place in God we are all looking for. He prayed:

"Show me your glory" (v. 18).

Let us pause for a moment. Had not Moses already seen the glory of God, streaming like a pavement of sapphire throughout the heavens and over all the earth (Exodus 24:10)? Yes, he had. But Moses wanted more—*more of God Himself.*

When we receive a gift from someone we experience their blessing. They do not have to be present for us to receive the gift or the happiness and satisfaction it gives. That is also the way it is with answered prayer. We can receive the blessing of happiness and satisfaction of the answer even if we do not sense the presence of the Giver.

For many of us, this is the end of prayer: to get what we want from God...and then to go on our way without Him. Not so for Moses. "Now show me your *glory.*"

You see, the Giver does not need to be present in order for us to receive the gift. He may be somewhere far away from us while we unwrap the delightful thing we asked for, but where there is glory— God himself is there in fullness!

COMING REVIVAL

Throughout the country we are hearing about revival and how it is happening among diverse groups of people. Those who can tell you how revival really came, however, are those who have paid a price. Now, for God to show you His glory, you have to do what

Moses did. You have to turn away even great blessings if God Himself is not in them. If you miss the place where the glory is revealed, you will not see it. If you are satisfied with the gift and will forego His presence, then you will miss the experience of walking in the revelation of His glory.

When the glory is seen, then the people of God are encouraged to open the gates wide and allow the King of glory to come in! You see, that is what God wants in these last days. Many are saying, "God will do signs and wonders as never before!" That may be so. But far more than that, *God wants to manifest Himself in glory in ways we've never seen before.*

God is searching hearts today, looking for men and women who will pray, "Lord, show me your glory."

Let me tell you something: In these last days, God is going to go beyond what we know to be normal, and He is going to do the incredible. Why? Because even if they do not know what they are hungering for, people are hungry for God himself. They will not settle for anything less.

This is why God is looking today for men and women who pray for more than self-indulging answers to prayer and for personal blessings, necessary as they are. He is looking for men and women who will pray, "Lord, show me your glory. For where your glory is— *you* are there. And I long to be with you!"

"Fine," the Lord replied. "But If I am going to revive you, I am also going to then lead you to someplace that is much farther than you have ever gone before."

FARTHER THAN EVER BEFORE

The Bible shows us over and over again that the men and women who have found a deeper place in God are those who have learned to be led by the Spirit. They became sons and daughters of God, in fact, because they allowed themselves to be led. You see, if God cannot lead you, you are not acting like His child. We know we are His children when our spirit bears witness with His Spirit that we are His children—because His life is being manifested through our lives.

To experience the depths of God we have to be willing to be led somewhere we've never been before.

Every one of us who wants to experience the depths of God in prayer—and not just a few answers to prayer—has to take on a new attitude. *We have to be willing to be led.* At some point we have to be willing to let Him lead us somewhere we've never been before. We have to stretch out our hand and say, "I don't know where I am, or where you are taking me, but I know there is a place of glory in you called *there*—and *there* is where I want to go."

For many of us, this means putting aside our beliefs about the way things are "supposed to be" when God comes into our lives. We imagine finding every kind of satisfaction we can imagine. Blessings. Settledness. Peace. Light on our path at all times. All the images our mind acquires about "life in God"—even those things can hinder us in the journey God is trying to take us on.

When we place our hand in God's hand in prayer and say, "Lead"—then we will find the place in Him that is more deeply satisfying than the level on which we live today. For God is breaking new ground, and He wants to take us into areas where we've never been before. This includes places where previously we have not allowed, and have even refused to let Him take us.

WHAT IS HOLDING YOU BACK?

Now many of us are held back from following God into the place of His glory by our own imaginations. We have a mental picture of "the way my life is supposed to be." That picture usually includes all the good things we've ever hoped for in this life. We thought that because we live in the affluent West we were guaranteed to achieve our dreams. When we became believers, many of us became even more certain we would get everything our hearts desired. We had God himself on our side, with all the power to make our dreams come true. Our materialism and desire for success and personal happiness, however, is not all that holds us back.

Many of us are held back by the friends we keep. You see, associations often lead us into places we never thought we would go. A man said to me recently, "Every time I meet a new group of people, whether it's at work or in a new church, I always meet the cynics." As he talked about his experience it was clear he had no idea why this phenomenon took place. He imagined it was just a strange coincidence that he found himself surrounded by people whose doubts and negative viewpoints kept them at a reserved distance from everyone else. He could not see that this happened every time because he himself was open to cynical views, and that he had a subtly superior idea of his own viewpoint.

Yes, associations will take you to places you didn't think you could go. If you hang around the wrong people together you will influence each other to go in the wrong directions—especially into worldliness. By contrast, of course, if you hang around those who are led by God's Spirit, they will take you to where God is.

Some of us are held back by one of the most difficult roadblocks there is in the spiritual life—and that is *unbelief.* We need to look at this problem more closely.

"Show me, and then I'll believe."

Jesus had told His disciples, "I am the Way, the Truth, and the Life" (John 14:10). He told them many other things, including the fact that He was to be betrayed unto death, that He would die on the Cross, and also that He would rise from the grave. Through all this, He said to them, *"Follow me"* (Matthew 8:22). Thomas, the disciple, was among those who heard all these things—and not only that, he also saw all the miracles Jesus performed to prove He had the spiritual authority to make these claims.

> *To experience the depths of God we have to be willing to be led somewhere we've never been before.*

Notwithstanding, Jesus' mighty works did not cause a certain man among His disciples to fully recognize Him as Lord.

At the end of John's Gospel, in Chapter 20, we find the disciples huddled in an upper room, hiding in fear of the Jewish leaders. They are discussing Jesus' resurrection, for many of them say they have seen Him alive after He was dead. But Thomas was not among those who had seen the Lord, and he had a problem believing their witness. He said, *"Unless I see the nail marks in his hands and put my fingers where the nails were, and put my hand into His side, I will not believe it"* (v. 25).

> *The Spirit of God can do things the mind of man cannot fathom.*

Suddenly, Jesus was standing there among them. But it was impossible. The doors were locked, and to get in He would have to have come *through* a solid object. Yet there He was, not a ghostly apparition, but Jesus of Nazareth, who had died, now alive and in the flesh.

Amazingly, Jesus singled Thomas out. Come here, He told him, and—if this is what it takes for you to believe—put your fingers in my side. Thomas reached out His hand, touched the warm, living flesh of Jesus, and all unbelief vanished:

Thomas said to him, "My Lord and my God!" Then Jesus told him, "Because you have seen me, you have believed; blessed are those who have not seen and yet have believed."
—John 20:28-29

Then John goes on to report something else that is very interesting:

Jesus did many other miraculous signs in the presence of his disciples, which are not recorded in this book. But these are written that you may believe that Jesus is the Christ, the Son of God, and that by believing you may have life in his name (vv. 30-31).

Do you realize the great and wonderful truth revealed to us in this passage? Though Jesus performed many miracles before His death that the four Gospel writers recorded, He performed many more miracles and on a greater scale after His resurrection. By doing so, He convinced the disciples that He is indeed the Lord—the One Who was, Who is, and Who is to come. That is why they were willing to be killed for their convictions. They had found something that is worth dying for. One would be a fool to give one's life otherwise. The power of Jesus influenced them so much that they performed great miracles and in the end their death confirmed their calling.

And yet.... Look at the trouble many of us have believing Jesus based on the things we are told He did before His resurrection. We read the great witness of these men who gave their lives for Christ because of what they saw Him do...and yet we struggle.

May I suggest something to you?

FOLLOWING GOD—WITHOUT LIMITS

If you want to learn how to really pray—that is, to pray in a way that will cause you to experience God—you have got to learn to do so without setting limits on Him. You must stop limiting Him by praying only for what you want and think you need. You have to stop praying for just the small things which, if God does not produce them in His way, you can produce for yourself anyway. You have to stop limiting God by your small perceptions of Who He is and what He can and cannot do. The God Who was crucified, died, and buried, is the God who rose on the third day. He is the Word of power and life—a Word that could not be silenced, not even by the grave. Believing His Word to us is the only way for us to enter into the glory of God.

You see, the Spirit of God can do things so glorious that the mind of man cannot fathom them. God does things that are strange to us. He makes donkeys talk. He is merciful to terrible people. He is a strange God. God also does things that are awesome to us. When we say awesome we must also include "aw-ful" because God not only does good things He does things that are, in their way, terrible. He not only builds up and creates, He tears down and destroys. He takes the foolish things of this world and uses them to confound the wise. He is amazing in all His ways. He is, in every sense, an awesome God.

What are these prayers we offer? Have you ever stopped to listen to what you are praying? Are they prayers offered in the flesh—seeking only fleshly, physical, earthly blessings? Or are they prayers offered in the Spirit—that is, offered in the Spirit that wants to reveal Who God is in all His awesome glory?

You see, those who know how to touch the heart of God in prayer are those who do not limit God by living and praying only in the realm of the flesh. By that I mean, we only ask for what we can see, or imagine on our own. Instead, we need to depend on the Spirit, and ask boldly for God to accomplish things that are impossible for the flesh to do or even imagine. In this way, we begin to follow God by praying in the Spirit—for the Spirit must tell the infirm flesh what to pray (see Romans 8:26)—calling out to Him *in prayer to manifest His glory in all the earth.*

May I say to you that so many of us—even God's own people—have never learned to walk beyond the realm of the flesh. The only realm that they are comfortable with and satisfied with is the realm of the flesh. And so we pray in the flesh, for things of the flesh. We may try to spice it up and make it sound spiritual, but we do not move one step in the Spirit toward that place in God where His glory is made manifest to us or anyone else.

Brothers and sisters, we have been swimming in the shallow end of the river of God far too long. It is time to move out into the depths. For as the psalmist wrote, *"Deep calls out to deep"* (42:7).

A Place in Prayer

Are you frustrated in your prayer life? Do your prayers seem powerless? Does God seem to be distant, and as if He is not listening?

There is a place in God in prayer. And in that place supernatural things happen. But you must be willing to go there, not just to get your personal needs met for your own satisfaction but to meet the God whose glory is the satisfaction of the whole earth.

> *Those who touch the heart of God in prayer are those who do not limit Him.*

I believe the time has come, and now is, when God wants to do supernatural things in our midst. The question is, are we ready to be vessels of prayer? Are we ready for the glory of God to be manifested?

When you find that place in God in prayer—you and your life will be transformed.

When you try to reach this place in God in prayer—I must warn you—it will be a fight. Your flesh, your mind, your old experiences, your perception, your attitude—none of these forces of the flesh want you to go there. It means leaving them behind and going farther, in spirit, than you have gone before.

When you find the place in the Lord—when you meet with God and see His glory—you will be transformed. There will be a radiance of God upon your face, as your spiritual countenance will be a reflection of God. People who know you will see you differently because they will see the glory of God upon you. Not everyone will like or appreciate it, however. Religious people hate it because a religious demon is stronger than sin. Sinners hate it because it convicts them of their sin.

MORE THAN WE ASKED FOR

You see, when most of us come to prayer all we want is a simple answer. And not just any answer, of course. We only want a "yes" from God. But the Bible tells us God is able to do "immeasurably more than we can ask or imagine" (Ephesians 3:20).

We do not imagine, you and I, that when we seek God in prayer what He wants to do is to show us His glory, to lead us in His ways, and in so doing transform everything about us.

That is God's design for prayer, and His end goal. Not just to give us small answers, little "tokens" of love, but to transform us. This is truly more than we asked for or imagined.

God is ready to take you to that place in prayer. Are you willing? Don't let your mind snare you when your prayers are not answered—don't get stuck in your doubts and questions. Enter deeper into prayer in His Spirit. God is trying to pull you out of the mire of human understanding, in which you are stuck. Don't resist Him. Likewise, don't let your soul snare you, tangling you in anger, sadness, or self-pity when what you ask for is not granted. God is trying to pull you out of the quicksand of your human soul, to save you from the tyrant of that little false god—which is you. Through all these afflictions of unanswered prayer, God delivers us from our selves. Do not break in spirit under this loving affliction. Be steadfast and patient in prayer, until God delivers you.

There is a place in God in prayer—*a place called there* if we are bold enough and determined enough we will reach that place. In that place God leads us in glory.

We cannot know what God will make of us, and make of our lives until we go to that place with Him in prayer. It is there where we see His glorious vision for our lives. When we have discovered that place in prayer, our strength is renewed like the eagle's—for we can patiently wait in Him as He brings to pass all things that concern us. God's anointing is in that place. His comfort, healing, and hope are in that place, too—as much as we need.

Best of all, as God meets us in this place of prayer—to heal us, lead us, and anoint us for the purpose of carrying out His mission in our lives—it is no longer our puny idea of glory that shines from us. What shines from us then is the glory of God Himself. For He longs not just to answer our prayers, but to share in and see His glory revealed in us. *That is when we have revival and resurrection life is flowing from the fullness of God into us.*

Beyond all your hopes, beyond every wish contained in your prayers, isn't this what you really long for—the life of God, lived out in you?

"Yes, Lord!" and "No, Lord!"

Perhaps you are saying, "Yes, Lord! There are many things I long for and seek you for in prayer. But this is what I really want—your fullness in me."

Perhaps you are saying, "No, Lord. As much as I want you, there are things that are dear to my heart and I long for them. Can't I just have you *and* these things?"

Whatever our answer may be, there is a deeper work which God must do in our lives so that we, His children, may walk with Him in truth. For that is His great desire (see 3 John 4). As one great saint put it, "The truth will make you free—but first, it may make you uncomfortable."

> *When you find that place in God in prayer you and your life will be transformed.*

You see, whether we willingly surrender to the Lord or struggle against His will, when God comes into our lives things may become difficult. Suddenly, life does not go the way we planned. In fact, you may come to wonder how someone who prayed so fervently came to be in such a place of confusion and darkness. How you came to feel so forsaken and alone.

Many believers have had to pass through this difficult, trying darkness on the way to the place in God called *there*. And it is to this time of trial that we must now turn our attention.

Chapter Four

A PLACE...IN DARKNESS

"**I** have almost lost my way."

"God has left me, and I feel as though I'm wandering in a spiritual wilderness."

"It's as if the light of my faith has gone out, and I'm in darkness—a place that seems even darker than where I was before I came to Christ."

These are statements I, and many other ministers of the gospel, hear from many people who have been faithful followers of God. We hear this from people who are, perhaps, not so desperate.

"I'm very confused, Dr. Fletcher. Everything was going along fine. And then suddenly my whole life went into turmoil. How could God have let this happen?"

"I have followed God for years—but then suddenly God stopped answering my prayers. And now I feel so much deep doubt and conflict in my spirit."

Sometimes I have even heard these words from men and women who were spiritual leaders as well as from everyday believers who were following hard after God. It is because they were following so hard after God that their anguish is so deep.

What is God about when we who are seeking Him find ourselves losing our way in the half-light of doubt and confusion…or wandering in a place where the light of faith is all but snuffed out and we feel we're in darkness?

PAUL, OUR WITNESS

If anyone may be considered a spiritual giant, it is Paul. He was the great apostle to the Gentiles, and the writer of so many of the New Testament letters to the churches. When Paul left Judaism behind and became a follower of Christ, he knew what was ahead for him. *Persecution for certain—and possibly even death*. He knew this, because he had been a persecutor of believers. He had watched Stephen be stoned (see Acts 8:1). Paul embraced these possibilities fully when he became a follower of Jesus Christ, serving him with even more zeal than he had when his heart was set against Christ.

> *Sometimes we must go through spiritual territory that is dark, and our souls feel benighted.*

And yet, there is one difficulty Paul most likely did not anticipate. That is, that he would have to pass through a place of spiritual darkness where he found himself all but cut-off from the One whom he had faithfully pursued with all his heart, soul, and strength. For he bares his soul in a moment of confession, saying, *"We were under great pressure* [in Asia Minor], *far more than we could endure, so that we despaired even of life. Indeed, in our hearts we felt the sentence of death"* (2 Corinthians 1:8-9a).

Do you hear what he is telling us? Paul, the pillar of churches throughout a whole sub-continent, admits that the light inside him had been nearly extinguished. He experienced that state of inner blackness that is utterly numbing to the soul, so much so he felt all but dead.

But now.... here is Paul, now on the other side of this experience. And now he sees a purpose even for the darkness. He writes, *"But this happened that we might not rely on ourselves but on God, who raises the dead....On Him we have set our hope, that he might continue to deliver us..."* (vv. 9b-10).

This gives a different perspective to one of Paul's statements many of us love to quote when we discuss discipleship and what is required when we follow after God. I am referring to a famous statement in Philippians, where Paul says, *"But whatever was to my profit I now consider loss for the sake of Christ. What is more, I consider everything a loss compared to the surpassing greatness of knowing Christ Jesus my Lord, for whose sake I have lost all things. I consider them rubbish, that I may gain Christ and be found in him"* (3:7-9).

I believe that what Paul was saying to the church at Philippi, and to us, is that nothing is as important in life as finding that place in God our souls long for and to which He calls us. Given what Paul has told us about his time of despair, I believe he is also acknowledging that sometimes we must go through spiritual territory that is dark and our souls feel benighted. No doubt, while Paul was struggling through despair, it must have seemed like an impossible barrier to get through. On the far side of it, however, he in effect tells us,

"If this is what was required to reach the place in God where I am now, even passing through great darkness and anguish of soul was worth it."

For Paul wrote, in what to me is the most important statement in the chapter, *"I want to know Christ and the power of his resurrection, becoming like him in his death"* (v. 10, emphasis added).

LIKE CHRIST IN HIS DEATH

Many of us seek God. We want life to be good, and we know God holds the power of blessing. Some of us even want to follow Christ. We know He holds the keys of heaven. But then the Way gets narrower. God calls us to follow Christ into the secret place where He welcomes only His intimate friends. And the passage leads through a spiritual territory no flesh wants to cross through. Death.

In order to come to that place in God, we must go through the annihilation of our self. Jesus Christ went through it, abandoning himself to the Cross and the grave and separation from God. If the very Son of God was made to walk this way in spirit, why would we think we should be spared?

The question is, why must we pass through such ordeals on the way to the secret place in God? Is it because He wants to test our faith—to see if we are really that faithful after all? Or is it because God wants us to suffer to pay some ultimate price in order to become most intimate with Him. God forbid we should think that way of Him.

Paul tells us why God does this, *"...to redeem us from all wickedness and to purify for himself a people that are his very own, eager to do what is good"* (Titus 2:14).

Only when we are purified of all our fleshly, and even wicked, motives do we become eager to do what is good—that is, the perfect will of God. Only then, can we be empowered by a kind of glory and grace, about which few of us know anything. And even fewer of us, with all our goodness, even come close to experiencing it.

Paul, by going through great darkness and purging of soul, found himself in a place in God where the glory of God was amazingly manifested in him. After his time of purging, we learn that Paul was so anointed with the glory of God people were healed just by touching handkerchiefs or aprons the he had touched (see Acts 19:12).

To get the full effect of the transformation that has happened here, we must understand how far Paul had come in his spiritual journey into God. Looking back from our viewpoint today, we may only see Paul as a spiritual giant. But that is not at all where Paul began. As a young man, Paul hated Christ and was His sworn enemy. He persecuted the body of Christ with a terrible vengeance. He had no connection whatever to what God was saying and doing by His Spirit. In fact, he wanted to stop what the Spirit of God was doing!

> *Only when we are purified of our fleshly motives are we eager to do the perfect will of God.*

Yet, this same Paul is the one who was later so full of the anointing of God that to come near him, to touch his garment, was to be jolted into divine health. *That* is evidence of transformation! This man, who once did not even believe in Jesus, was radically changed because he was willing to pass through the darkness that stops most of us. He was willing to go through even that terrible deadness of soul known as despair if that was what it took *"to know Him in the power of His resurrection"* (Philippians 3:10).

BEYOND ALL EARTHLY POWERS

> *You cannot have a long-distance relationship with God and expect close-up results.*

Some critics of Christianity say, "You Christians—you don't even know how to enjoy life. All you think about is death and heaven." But they say this because they do not understand that there is *another kind of life* promised to us. A kind of life from within, that satisfies in ways this fleshly and temporary life never can. It was for this—*the power of resurrection life*—that Paul longed. It was for this experience that Paul bore up under every hardship and endured the spiritual darkness of despair.

He surrendered himself so as to experience this power that is beyond every earthly power. Paul was only following in the footsteps of Christ Jesus himself. The Bible tells us it was *"for the joy set before Him"* that Jesus endured the Cross and death (see Hebrews 12:2). This is one of Jesus' most powerful revelations to us—that beyond all death, and every kind of death, lies the power of life eternal.

Why is this revelation so vital? For this reason: When we know that we know that we know there is power in God to resurrect us and fill us with life again no matter what we go through, then even problems that used to be major take on a different hue. We see "big problems" from a new viewpoint, and they become *little problems*. What used to wipe us out no longer overwhelms us. No longer do we throw our hands up and cry, "God, where are you?"

The kind of life that comes from God is all wrapped up in Jesus' resurrection.

Paul, like Jesus himself, knew that he had to go *beyond* where many of us today *stop*. Today, we talk a lot about "the presence" of God. We say, "Seek God's presence." And now "the presence" has become a kind of buzz-word. But why is it many of us have been going into His presence for a long time...but we have no joy?

Paul wanted to know what was beyond the presence. He wanted to get hold of the power of the resurrection, which Jesus knew. Let me tell you something: The life that comes from God is all wrapped up in Jesus' resurrection. Paul said, I want to go beyond death and the grave to know resurrection power.

You see, there are many people who come to the presence of God but they don't get the real picture. When Jesus Christ rose again from the dead, He made it very clear to all His disciples that His position had changed. Now He was their Savior—but even more than that He was about to be crowned by the Father, as King and Lord. That is why, when Mary came looking for Jesus, wanting to touch Him, He said, "No, you can't touch me now." After conquering death, He was preparing to be King of All Kings—acknowledged by God himself as the Lord of Life, that is, the One Who is Above and Beyond All Earthly Powers. When it comes to kings and great lords, you don't touch them, you just do what they say. Mary understood this, because when she left the presence of this King of Kings and Lord of Life she went out full of joy, and ran trembling to do His word. All of the purposes she had come with were swallowed up, destroyed, dead and left behind in a grave—because now she had seen Christ in His resurrection power and from that moment on the very reason for her existence had changed profoundly.

Many of us seek the presence because we want the Lord Jesus to patch up the old life we have. We may even want to thank and praise Him for being our Savior. But what is the point, I ask you, of seeking the presence of the King of Kings and Lord of Life if you do not come with a spirit that is willing to let all your old desires and motives die? Die, so that you may become *ready to go beyond that death into the resurrection life He wants to give you?*

To follow Christ Jesus into death, and beyond death to resurrection life means to come into His presence *ready to do whatever He tells you to do.* Only then have you allowed the life that lies beyond death and the power that is beyond all earthly powers to enter.

OUR CHOICE

In every relationship, there is a choice to be made, and in our relationship with Jesus, our King and Lord, it is no different. We can choose to be close to Him—willing to be where He is and do what He is doing. Or we can choose to be distant—willing to do just what we want to do, whether He is interested in it or not.

Most of us want a relationship with God, but we choose to have a distant one—while all the time we want to get the benefits of closeness. Many of us have the attitude that goes something like this: "God, you know you love me and I love you. But you stay in your place and I'll stay in my place. When I think we can hook up, we'll hook up. When I think I need you, I will come. When you think you need me, give me a call...but just don't come over without giving me fair warning. Let me know you are coming, so I can see if it's a good day for you to come or not. If you have something you'd like me to do, give me lots of advance time to think and pray about it. I'll need to figure out how to do what you want me to do while still allowing myself room to do what I want to do."

Today, we have a form of spiritual insanity. We have servants telling the King what they will and will not do.

Yes, most of us have a long-distance relationship with God, but we want close-relationship results. Because we become so occupied with receiving warm-fuzzy feelings from being in His presence, we see less of a continual move of God. He wants to take us beyond His presence, through death, and into resurrection life in Him.

Once again, there are those of us who say, "I am not going to rest until I experience the deep things of God. I am willing to let go. I am willing to drop certain things in my life that are holding me back. There are some things that have crept into my life over the years and I am willing to let them go. I am even willing to let go of my understanding about God, to let Him teach me new things. I want to get the real stuff. I want something from God I have never had before."

I say: "Is that really so?"

The only attitude that will be acceptable is the one demonstrated by Paul. He said, in effect, *"I want to know God so badly that I am willing to take everything I considered to be gain and get rid of it"* (see Philippians 3:8).

> *To find the place in God called there you will have to go through the darkness with God.*

Paul was an accomplice to the murder of an innocent man—Stephen—and yet he experienced God in a way we have never experienced Him. When he walked into a city, the power of God would fall and there would be revival and great joy. Paul would just walk into town and the demon possessed would recognize who he was and in Whose company he walked. "Behold, the servant of the living God!" they'd shout. And Paul would turn around and rebuke those evil spirits and they would come flying out and be cast into the pit.

What is the difference between Paul and us? Why was this man able to experience more than what the Church today has been experiencing? It is because Paul made a choice: it was to let God give the orders—to let every choice be God's choice.

MANIA IN THE CHURCH

Many of you may not like what I have to say next. But it must be spoken.

When God is not really moving in our midst in the way He promised to move, I believe we become embarrassed. To cover up our embarrassment, I believe we begin to make up things like "moves of God" and "spiritual giftings." Because we are so gullible and desperate for God, we not only make them up but we believe them and start to act as if they are the real thing. I suppose we do this in an attempt to confirm to ourselves that God is in our midst, and that the things we are believing in or holding onto are working. Yet it is make-believe and not the real thing.

Today, for instance, some believers have made up a whole theology—or rather, call it a "demonology." Perhaps you have encountered these people. In some circles today, everything is a demon. There is a demon for everything—a demon of coffee, a demon of ice cream.... In this demonology, you ask God to tell you the demon's name and He is supposed to tell you: "Demon of Laziness," or "Demon of Too Much TV." Then you are supposed to name this demon and drive him out.

I think it is amazing how God seems to talk to people who never even come to His presence, let alone press on like Paul following Jesus in His death and resurrection. Nevertheless, these people will tell you, "The Lord told me this..." and "The Lord told me to do that...".

"The Lord told me I am to go out and perform signs and wonders." Very well then, I say, let's go and pray and seek God, as Jesus our Lord did. "Well, Dr. Fletcher, I don't know. The Lord did not tell me I should go pray."

"The Lord told me to minister in prophetic words. He told me I am supposed to be a prophet." Then let us fast and repent for the people, so their hard hearts will be softened to receive the correction and guidance of the Lord. "Sorry, Dr. Fletcher, I already fasted...once, I think."

"The Lord told me that I will have the power to pray for ten people to rise from the dead." "That is fantastic," I say, "but before that let's go out and win souls that are now dead to God." Then comes the response, "No, Brother, that is not my ministry. That's for the evangelists."

Once again, it's amazing that God always tells these people how to perform miraculous signs—though usually they are of the kind which cannot be proven or disproven. Apparently, He never tells them, "Follow my Son Jesus to the Cross... and beyond the Cross to the grave. Come when you are good and dead, and then we'll start over with a new kind of life."

Today, we have a form of spiritual insanity. We have servants telling the King what they will and will not do.

Today, we have a kind of mania in the Church—a spiritual form of insanity. We have the servants telling the King what they will and will not do. We have believers who are very much alive to their own egos and desires and wills...and very dead to the will of the Lord. We have selected what we want, and we have packaged it, and then we have found preachers who will actually confirm to us what we want.

When Paul entered into God's presence, the first thing he said was, "What do you want me to do?" Whenever you experience God's presence, it is easy to feel the thrill of excitement. But it is a bit more tricky to let go of your agenda and listen for what He will tell you to do.

If we want more than the presence of God, if we want to know Him in the power of resurrection life, it will have to be "more of Him, less of us." We will have to follow hard after Him, and send our own hearts' desires to the Cross. We must pass through the darkness of spiritual death to our selves. When we have come as close to God as we can—finding that place in Him in the darkness—then it will be impossible not to experience His fullness in glory and power.

What Do You Really Want?

Let me ask—do you really want more of God? Do you want to find the place in Him called *there?*

If you genuinely want more of God, then would you be willing to do at least one of the things He asked you to do...and do it joyfully?

"That I may know Him," said Paul. Nothing else mattered to Paul; nothing was so dear to his heart. He wanted to put all of his energy and full commitment into serving the Lord.

When you are determined to do something, you go after it with zeal. You say "no" to anything and everything that distracts you. You give up some things, and discipline yourself not to do others. You don't think of it this way, but you are going through a type of death. You are "dying" to things that are of lesser importance to you. They have no hold on you. And at the same time you pursue your goal with all your body, mind, soul, and strength. When you are pursuing the thing you love, you can lose all track of time and the whole world can recede into the distance. You are caught up, and totally focused, on the thing you love.

What is that *thing* for you—that object of your desire? Is it making more money? Golf? Gazing into the eyes of the man or woman you love? Some hobby or simple escape? Is it getting "high" on some feeling, "spiritual" or otherwise?

Why do we not put the same determination into seeking God, so that we pass through the death of lesser dreams and drives and find the resurrection life in Him that is beyond all death and all earthly powers? Why do we not put the same energy into knowing and doing the things of God?

LIFE BEYOND

If you really want to experience the kind of life that is beyond this life, and experience it now—ask God for more. And make yourself available to Him, saying, "Lord, when I experience more of you, I will make your glory known to the world. I will not try to hoard it for myself."

Tell Him, "God, I want more of you. I want your fullness."

He says, "When you are ready to be empty of yourself, then you are available. Then I can share my glory with you."

God is saying to us, His people, "I have called many—but only a few make themselves available to be the chosen." The chosen are those who, like Paul, are willing to share with Him in His death—that is, death to lesser things, that we might know the greater things of God.

How about you? Are you going to be among those who go beyond death, to resurrection life? Will you be among those who prove themselves to be chosen?

THE COST

If you want that place in the fullness of God, it is going to cost you something. It is going to cost you your excuses. It is going to cost you your fear. It is going to cost you the very things you don't want to give up, because experiencing the fullness of God requires us to move with Him as He moves and to do the things He asks us to do.

To find the place in God called *there*, you will have to go through the darkness with God. As the psalmist has promised us (see Psalm 18:11), beyond every awful darkness we may pass through, God *is* indeed *there*.

> *The kind of life that comes from God is all wrapped up in Jesus' resurrection.*

Chapter Five

A Place...in Serving

A gentleman told me this unhappy story recently.

"I came to the Lord as a teenager, through a high school campus ministry. They emphasized that Jesus was our friend. The churches I went to talked about Jesus as Savior and Lord, of course, but mainly they had the same emphasis—'Jesus is our friend.'

"As I grew up and went on to serve God—both on my job as a business executive and through my church as a men's group leader— I emphasized the same thing. I would tell people, 'Jesus wants to help you. He loved you enough to die on the Cross for you. Let Him be your friend.'

"I didn't notice, however, the effect this mindset was having on me," he said, sadly. "Over time I became lax about my ethics. I would cheat a little here and tell half the truth there. All the while I was attending church, leading a ministry, and tithing, of course. I never noticed the erosion going on in my soul because I kept telling myself, 'Jesus is my friend. He understands that I'm only human.' I didn't see the bigger problem for a minute."

With deep sorrow in his eyes, he told me, "One day I crossed another line. A younger woman at work had lost her husband in a tragic motorcycle accident. Our friendship began when I offered to pray for her. It is very ironic that there was only a few months between my 'spiritual ministry' to her and the affair we had. In the end, when the Spirit convicted me of my sin, the after-effects were terrible. She fell apart, claiming I'd taken advantage of her vulnerable emotional condition. My wife figured out what was going on. Though she has stuck with me, she was devastated—and our marriage is so deeply wounded I believe it will take years to repair.

"I know that what I did is nobody's fault but my own," he concluded. "But I know that it came about in part because I was living my spiritual life on a weak foundation. I believed that Jesus was first and foremost a *friend*. I treated His words—His commands—as if they were the opinions of a friend, and not the commandments of my Lord.

> *A servant must earn his master's trust. In time, he may even become an intimate friend.*

"Because of this mindset I lost my footing. I lost my direction. I thought I was safe 'in Christ,' but I was really only into my self. Spiritually, I was not in God at all. I was no place."

I wonder if, in all his years as a Christian, this man never heard anyone preach or teach from Jesus' powerful message recorded for us near the end of John's Gospel. I believe it would have made all the difference...if He had received and understood this one crucial truth.

A BIG "IF"

As His earthly ministry was coming to an end, Jesus said to His disciples, *"You are my friends if you do what I command"* (John 15:14).

You see, we get the conditions under which we experience God's love confused with conditions under which we experience His true friendship. God's love is unconditional. His mercy is offered to us all the time, for everything. But God's friendship—now that is another matter. Certain conditions apply. And when it comes down to it, friendship with God is not like friendship with anyone else.

Because we have not been taught well on this subject, many believers—perhaps even *most* believers—are confused. Are we *friends?* Or are we *servants?* And because we don't know how to make sense of this matter, few Christians find their way to that place we can reach in God where purpose and joy lie—that is, a place in serving.

SERVANTS *AND* FRIENDS

What is friendship with God like? What are the conditions under which God calls us His "friends?" How can we be friends if we are called to serve Him?

Jesus spoke of these things with His disciples, and in that same passage at the end of John's Gospel we read: "I no longer call you servants, because a servant does not know his master's business. Instead, I have called you friends, for everything that I learned from my Father I have made known to you. You did not choose me, but I chose you and appointed you to go and bear fruit, fruit that will last" (15: 15-16a).

We can begin to make sense of what Jesus is telling us here if we consider the way it is when we have someone who serves us. As a simple example, let's say you have a favorite restaurant where you have dined for years. At this restaurant you may have a favorite serving person. He or she is very pleasant and attentive, and very quickly comes to know your needs, wants, likes and dislikes. While you are still settling yourself in the chair he or she is at your side, saying, "May I bring you some of that iced tea you like so much—unsweetened and that special little twist of lemon?"

This waiter or waitress, in time, may gain your favor so much that you become relaxed enough to carry on more and more personal conversation. You may eventually discuss your personal health, the type of business you are in. On a day when you show up at the restaurant in an unhappy mood, you may even feel comfortable enough with this server to tell them a bit about your troubles. Or if they are not being their usual cheery self, you may say, "You seem a little down today. Is something wrong?"

Because this person has been attentive as a servant, you have come to like them. From that foundation you may even invite this kind of personal familiarity. They are still your servant—but the relationship has taken on some of the qualities of a friendship, as well. Perhaps if you meet them elsewhere sometime, in another setting, your relationship will shift even more and you will become true friends.

Do you see what I mean?—the very same person may occupy two roles at the same time: servant and friend.

Then there are servants who really become something more—something like an intimate friend. Not many of us have household servants, especially full-time helpers like butlers, cooks, or nannies.

But the relationship with servants like this can become even more like that of a friend.

At first, of course, you will be guarded with your household servant. You don't know them—how capable they really are, or how trustworthy. You are very careful about limiting the personal information you give them. That is because anything that is very personal you reserve to share with your most trusted friends. Why? Because a friend is someone who has proven to be trustworthy. You have taken some risks with them, and they did not let you down. They kept your private matters

> *The universe is out of order, when we think God must do what we ask.*

to themselves and did not spread gossip about you all over town. They protected you in confidential matters, and acted in your best interest. This servant has taken on the characteristics of an intimate friend. Many relationships like this—between servants and employers—also become friendships for life.

But wait, we have skipped over something. There are developmental stages and changes in the transformation from servanthood to friendship.

For instance, initially a servant may be warned not to go into certain areas of your home. Certain items may be off-limits—for instance, your purse or wallet. It may be some time before you send them into town to pick up something using your credit card. It may be an even longer time before you discuss more intimate details of your personal relationships and private financial or business affairs with them.

Eventually, if you do reach the point where you relax these limitations and place more confidence in your servant—in more areas of your life, trusting them to do more on your behalf, it will be for one reason and one reason only: *They have accomplished small tasks all along the way that have proven they are both capable and trustworthy. And in so doing, they have proven they have the character of a servant who is also a trusted friend.*

> *The true servant of the Lord asks, "How can I serve my master today?"*

After a servant has given the expected service faithfully for a reasonable period, trust is established between the two parties. There comes a freedom in communicating matters of the heart, and deeper issues can now be discussed. Now your servant is no longer just a servant. This also becomes true in our relationship with God.

You see, many of us are troubled in our relationship with God. We say, "God feels distant." Or "My spiritual life is stale. It's not going anywhere." Or even, "God has not done what I wanted, so I can't trust God."

However, the true facts are these: We have not been faithful in small things, so God cannot trust us with greater things. We may be free to dump the contents of our hearts in God's ear, but He cannot trust His heart to us. Maybe He cannot even truly call us servants because we have failed to act in obedience to His directives and commands. If He cannot qualify us as faithful servants, then He most certainly cannot call us friends. He cannot open to us the secret things that are kept in His heart.

CART BEFORE THE HORSE...AND NO HORSE!

I must tell you, what many of us call service to God is not much more than a token offering. In fact that is just what we do—give Him token offerings. We do little services and "favors" for God, calling it "service." At the same time we expect big pay-offs.

This is not servanthood. And it is nothing like true friendship. It is an arrangement of convenience. "If I do something for you...then you do something for me." It is conditional, and we usually set the conditions. "I will help this person..." or "I will be kind to that rotten so-and-so...". But then, God, you will need to do this and that for me." And the truth of the matter comes out when God tests the relationship by not doing this or that. Suddenly we see who is servant and who is master! "How could you let me down like this? What kind of God are you? After all I have done for you—how ungrateful. Out of my presence now. You are dismissed. I will get back to you when I am ready to talk to you again."

We think that we can set the conditions of our relationship with God! We imagine that we can call the shots, and He must do what we ask. We have the cart before the horse. But it is often even worse than that. We expect God to perform at our command, when we are not even willing to do anything He asks or commands us to do. When God gets in the cart expecting to be pulled—there is no horse!

Indeed the universe is out of order when we think this way. Or rather, our heads are out of order—scrambled. We need to clear up our way of thinking here. We need to get back to the arrangement God had in mind, and understand what it is God asks us to do as His servants. Then we need to get back to an understanding of the conditions under which we may be called His friends. Then we will have the cart and the horse in right order once again.

"THIS *IS MY COMMANDMENT*"

When Jesus sat His friends down for a last supper together before His crucifixion, He knew time was short. He knew there would be a time of confusion and sorrow for them. A time when they would feel lost. Then He would rise from the grave, to spend another short period of time with them. Then He would rise to the Father, there to receive His crown and take His place as King of kings and Lord of lords.

Jesus knew many other things, too—especially what lay ahead for His disciples...those living and those who were to come. He knew His disciples would be faced with all kinds of formulas and laws by which to show themselves to be "true believers." He knew that some of those rules would be erroneously presented as if they were "necessary regulations" which, if observed, would secure for them the pardon and the ransom which only His shed blood can ensure. He knew there would be terrible persecutions and trials that would make them struggle just to maintain faith at all. He knew there would be times of ease, when some of us would forget whose servants we were and slip into the role of master, mistakenly thinking that being a believer means having God to serve you.

Now when you know your time with someone is limited, especially with someone whom you want to carry out your wishes, you make your instructions clear, simple, and easy to follow. This is true of Jesus' words to His disciples just prior to his departure from this earth. He says to them, *"My command is this: Love each other as I have loved you"* (John 15:12).

What could be simpler? What could be clearer? God's mission was and is to pour out His life sacrificially for the salvation, healing, teaching, and instruction in righteousness to the whole world. Notice, He did not say, "Love each other when it feels good or its convenient." As God loved us, and continually loves us, showering us with grace, we are commanded to love each other *in the very same way.*

"Love each other" is God's shorthand instruction. "I am going away," says our Master, "and while I'm gone I want you to start by loving each other. If you forget everything else, don't forget this commandment. I'll repeat it—*Love each other.*"

You see, when we love as God loves, we will be carrying out His very specific commandment. The servant of God will be the one who looks about himself all day, every day, as he goes about his master's business, asking, "How can I serve my Lord and Master by loving today? How can I be a vessel of my Lord's grace to this person? How can I serve God in love by giving instruction in the kind of righteous living that keeps people from the ways of sin and pain and death?"

You see, this is the condition in which the servant proves himself or herself to be a trusted friend to the Master. You are my friends if you do what I command, says Jesus, " *Then* the Father will give you whatever you ask in my name" (John 15:16b, emphasis added).

Now we have the order and the relationship right. "I am the Master.

> *Many things remain secret in the heart of God because He finds few to whom He can entrust His burdens.*

You are the servants. You have done what is asked. And in so doing you have gained my trust. You have met the conditions in which a servant becomes a friend. Now what is it you were going to ask for?"

The thing is, of course, what you ask for when you think you are the master and what you ask for when you know you are a trusted servant are two very different things.

THE HEAVY HEART OF GOD

To reach a place in God in serving—a place in which you are treated as a beloved and trusted servant—is to hold a very honored position. In the Bible, we find that, say, cup-bearer of the king was a coveted and important position. Paul referred to himself as a "bondservant" of Christ (see Colossians 1:23).

Why is it an honor to be recognized by God as a beloved servant?

It is because, the Bible tells us in many places, God's heart is heavy. It is heavy with acts of mercy and healing, with fresh revelation and with correction for His children, and with acts of re-creation for the whole world. He is looking throughout the earth to find those with whom He can share the secret things that are heavy on His heart.

There are many secrets in the heart of God because He finds so few to whom He can trust the burdens of love He carries for us (see Deuteronomy 29:29). He has to find people He can trust. If God finds a trusted person, He will first make sure that He takes your side—that is, He comes to your level and begins to speak to you and say things to you that amaze you. Then He begins to invite you to where He lives.

When Jesus gave His great commandment to His disciples— "Love each other"—He has spent enough time with them to know their hearts. Yes, He knew there was more doubt and unbelief to be purged, but their relationship had been firmly established. This time they were no longer servants, so He wanted to make it clear to them what His most supreme wish was: "Love each other." If you do this, He told them, you will be doing the will of my Father.

God's love and His glory shine as one. He doesn't intend for His glory to remain in heaven. When Jesus came, the glory of God was in Him, but He did not intend to take the glory back. He intended to leave it here. That is why the anointing did not go with Jesus. It remained here, because the earth needs more work than heaven. For God had made it plain that He wants His glory—the perfection of all things—to fill the whole earth, as the waters cover the sea. (see Isaiah 11:9) There is much to be done in the world to manifest His glory. He is always looking for faithful people to accomplish His mighty and loving acts. He is looking for people to take on the anointing to help Him finish up the work that needs to be done.

No wonder Jesus said, "I tell you the truth, the Son can do nothing by himself; he can only do what He sees His Father in heaven doing, because whatever the Father does, the Son does" (John 15). Whatever I do, Jesus said, is the very intent of God. Whatever I say is the thing that God would say.

MORE THAN SERVANTS

To become a servant in the manner that Jesus was—that is the path we must travel if we desire to get to that place of oneness with God, and to that secret place that is in God.

> *He will take you to His secret chambers, and there we will be privileged to hear Him tell us what it is that lies heavy on His heart.*

When you have reached that place where you are doing and saying only what your Master would say and do, no longer will people see you. Instead they will see and hear the reflection of the Master in you. As Jesus said, *"If you really want to see God—just look at me. If you don't believe it, just see the works that I do. Are they not the words and deed that represent God himself? So I am no longer just a servant of God. I am just like Him. If you've seen me, you've seen Him."* (see John 14:6-14).

If God would open wide our spiritual eyes, we would understand the way our glorious and loving God wants to manifest Himself through us. Then perhaps we would know why it is so urgent for us to come to that place in God in serving where we become beloved servants in whom He can trust. Only then can He make us His intimates, sharing with us the secrets, burdens and intentions of His heart. I have seen video tapes of mighty servants of God, like Sister Kathryn Kuhlman, and have seen how they were mightily used of God. I notice that these men and women always make profound statements which many people fail to grasp. True servants of God will say something like, "The miracles you see being done here, I am not the one doing them. They are being done by the Lord working through me. They are the result of His anointing." And so, they say, "Don't put your eyes on me. Put your eyes on Jesus."

When is a servant more than a servant? When are they also a beloved friend of God? The answer is, when they listen until they understand His will...and then make themselves totally available so that His will may be done, by His power, through them. When they have made themselves available enough to God that others can see Him in them. When this happens for you and me, we will be able to say with Paul, *"It is no longer I who live, but Christ lives in me"* (Galatians 2:20).

"Come Away..."

Today, many say, God wants to pour out His anointing. This may be so. First, He wants to find men and women who have made their way to the place in God in serving before He pours out His anointing upon us and reveals His secrets to us.

Today if you and I will seek this place in serving, the Lord will see that we are serious in our desires. He will change His mind toward us, for in time we will become more than servants...we will also become His trusted friends. Then we will experience times when we are specially invited by God. We will hear His Spirit say, *"Come away with me"* (see Song of Songs 2:10). He will take you to His secret chambers, and there we will be privileged to hear Him tell us what it is that lies heavy on His heart.

Then we will join with Him, under the power of His anointing, in the joyful work of transforming the world...until the whole earth is, indeed, full of the glory of God, as the waters cover the sea.

Are you willing to join the King in His secret chambers? To hear the things He has on His heart? Are you willing to become more than a servant, but also a trusted friend?

The psalmist tells us, *"The Lord confides in those who fear Him"* (25:14).

God is raising up men and women whom He can trust with His anointing. He can trust us only when He knows we are trustworthy, eager, and longing to do His will. Many, many have been called, but few are willing—and therefore, few are chosen.

My prayer, as we close this chapter, is that we will choose to become trusted servants, men and women whom God can then also welcome as friends into His chambers. I pray that there, in that place in God, He will open our eyes and ears to perceive what He plans to do...among our families and friends...in our churches...in towns and cities...and in all the nations.

May He give us a vision of His glory spreading and His Word proceeding to every land throughout the earth. And may we see the part He wants us to play as trusted servants and beloved friends of the Most High God.

Amen and Amen!

Chapter Six

A Place...in God

W E have all heard stories, perhaps, about great men and women of God who have suddenly left the ministry or given up on faith altogether. Sometimes it throws us. How could someone who was so strong in the Lord turn back? How could they give up their place in God?

The truth is, there are many of us who believe we are following hard after God right now. We are experiencing times in His presence. We may even know moments when we are invited into the secret place—in prayer, in darkness, or as a beloved servant-friend to God. But the Bible is clear in its warning: *If you think you are standing firm, be careful that you don't fall!* (1 Corinthians 10:12).

Most of us are blind to the things that may make us stumble and lose our place in God. Sometimes we really do not see them. At other times we do see them out of the corner of our eye, as it were, but we choose to ignore the things that are endangering our walk in God.

> *Most of us are blind to the things that may make us stumble and lose our place in God.*

BIG THINGS...AND LITTLE THINGS

Recently, I heard of a man who had been a strong Christian leader in his city. Overnight, it seemed, he fell from grace. One day he packed up his things, left his wife and children, and moved in with the woman with whom he had been having an affair. It was not an "overnight" thing, of course. He had been seeing this woman secretly for a long time.

Later, when he repented and returned to the Lord, he admitted, "If I am honest, I have to say I saw it coming from the moment I met this woman. Our eyes locked, and I did not turn away. Every time I was in the room with this woman I kept looking to see if she was still looking. Every time I told myself, 'This is dangerous.' In fact, I believe the Holy Spirit in me was stirring my conscience, warning me. But I ignored the voice of the Lord.

"When I turned back to the Lord I truly had to confess, 'Lord, I have sinned against my wife and children, and against my friends. But mostly, I have sinned against you. Because you came to warn me about the danger I was in, and I cut you off. I treated you, my King and my Lord, with contempt. With all my heart, I am sorry.'"

> *To love the things of this world more than we love Him is to treat our gracious and merciful God with contempt.*

As deadly a ground as this man walked on—for it is deadly to ignore the Holy Spirit—there is a woman who is in similar spiritual danger, and she truly does not see it.

This woman was all smiles when she told me, "I had nothing and the

Lord blessed me with everything. When there was no way for me to afford a home, He opened the right doors, and now I live in a wonderful home—the house of my dreams, really. I praise Him and thank Him every day for my home."

It certainly sounded like her home was a wonderful blessing, bestowed upon her by our gracious God. But then, she added, "And if my house was taken away from me now somehow—by fire, or a financial setback—I don't think I could go on living. I love my house *that* much."

Amazingly, I know this sister in Christ did not see the most obvious thing—that her blessing had become an idol. You see, it was not that she might stop following God and lose her place in Him if something happened to her home. Her blessing had become an end in itself—and she had already stopped following after God in her spirit. She was no longer in that place in God where He wants His children to be.

What about you? Are you aware of obvious dangers that can lead you away from your place in God? What about the "little" things? And what about your "blessings?"

What *would* cause you to stumble, and leave your place in God?

All along, we have been talking about coming to a new and different place in God. A place in Spirit we would like to reach. This place is not just a place in seeking, prayer, darkness turned to light, or serving. It is the place where we are more fully present to God and He is more fully present to us in His love, power, and glory. In this place, there is less and less distance between us. We are moving toward that wonderful time when we will be joined to Him at the great marriage supper of the Lamb. (see Revelation 19) We all have an inborn tendency to hold back from God. No matter how long we have been in Him, no matter how exciting our experiences with His Spirit, we all have this tendency to let other things get between us. Sometimes we want to go to God. At other times we hold back, or resist Him. Even those of us who have sometimes experienced unspeakable intimacy and joy in God experience these times of withdrawal.

What is it within you that keeps you from wanting to *remain* in this place in God? And when we have experienced it—what keeps us from staying there? What are the things—big or small—that distract you and lead you away from God's presence?

"WHERE YOUR TREASURE IS...."

Jesus knew that we, His followers, would be hindered in our walk with God. He came to this earth, and inhabited flesh, and experienced all that we experience. He was well aware of our many distractions. And because He took on human nature, He also understood just how weak and easily led astray we are!

For this reason, in His gracious ministry to us, Jesus gave us a clear warning. We find it in the Sermon on the Mount. First He speaks of earthly distractions, telling us, *"Do not store up for yourselves treasures on earth, where moth and rust destroy, and where thieves break in and steal: But store up for yourselves treasures in heaven, where moth and rust do not destroy, and where thieves do not break in and steal: For where your treasure is, there your heart will be also"* (Matthew 6:19-21).

Here on earth our treasures can get rusty or moth-eaten, and also thieves can divest us of riches, but when we store our treasures in heaven, God makes sure that they are protected.

Then Jesus speaks about the effect on our spirit when we have made the things of this world and this life our treasure: *"The eye is the light of the body. If your eyes are good, your whole body will be full of light. But if your eyes are bad, your whole body will be full of darkness. If then the light within you is darkness, how great is that darkness. No one can serve two masters: either he will hate the one, and love the other; or he will be devoted to the one, and despise the other. You cannot serve both God and mammon"* (6: 22-24).

When we think of "mammon," some of us only equate that term with "money." But "mammon" is anything of this world that takes on the status of a god to us.

To love the things of this world more than we love Him is to treat our gracious and merciful God with contempt.

Jesus is plainly telling us several things. First, the more we fix our hearts on earthly things, allowing them to become "treasures," the greater our danger of being led away from our place in God. Second, He is telling us that these earthly treasures can shine so brightly they dazzle our eyes. Dazzled by the shiny objects of earth, our spiritual vision is made dark to God and the things of God.

> *When we become preoccupied with life and earthly things—even "things of the Lord"—and not occupied with the Lord himself, we have begun to backslide.*

When our spiritual perceptions become weak or darkened, Jesus warns us, we are truly headed into great darkness.

Most tragically, we can come to despise God. Though we would be horrified at the very idea that we "hate" God, to despitefully ignore One who has been so gracious, loving, and merciful to us, to treat His call to the place of intimacy as nothing—that is, indeed, hateful. The truth is, that to love the fleeting, decaying things of this world and this life more than we love God is to treat Him with nothing less than contempt.

"ALL THESE THINGS...."

Jesus, our blessed Savior, our King and Lord, is kind enough to tell us what "things" are a danger to us spiritually. What are the things of this world and of this life that can become false gods to us?

"I tell you, do not worry about your life, what you will eat, or drink.... Is not life more important than food...? Look at the birds of the air: they do not sow or reap, or store away in barns, and yet your heavenly Father feeds them. Are you not much more valuable than they? Who of you by worrying can add a single hour to his life?

"And why do you worry about clothes? See how the lilies of the fields grow; they do not labor or spin: Yet I tell you, that not even Solomon in all his splendor was dressed like one of these. If that is how God clothes the grass of the field, which is here today and tomorrow is thrown into the fire, will he not much more clothe you, O you of little faith?"

—Matthew 6:25-30

Has owning more things ever made you happier? Or has it just given you more things to worry about?

Jesus might have gone on to list the many, many things from which we seek comfort and security in life. I tell you—just look at all the advertisements on television and flip through the catalogs you receive daily in your junk-mail. There is your list of shiny treasures to distract you from God. When this parade of delightful junk comes before our eyes we become afraid that we are missing out on something everyone else is enjoying. We cannot stand the thought that someone else is happier than we are. We worry, not so much that we are not going to have the basics of life—food and clothes— we worry that we are going to miss out on "the better things" in life. Why should everyone else enjoy nice things, we worry, when we don't have them?

Knowing our hearts, knowing this about us, Jesus goes on to say,

"So do not worry saying, what shall we eat? or, what shall we drink? or, what shall we wear? For the pagans run after all these things, and your heavenly Father knows that you need them."
—Matthew 6:31,32

That is to say, God knows our basic needs. In fact, He knows us so well He knows we are actually better off, and quite happy, if our lives are simple and we are not saddled with so many earthly things to care for. I ask you—has owning more things ever really made you happier, or has it just given you more to worry about?

Truly, you and I do not need much more than food and cloth-ing to make us happy... if we have a kind of life and joy that come from a place outside this world. This is why Jesus tells us from the very start where to find this kind of life and joy. He tells us, instead, to start storing up our treasures in heaven (6:20). To do so, we must *"…seek first the kingdom of God and his righteousness, and all these things will be given to you as well"* (6:33).

OUR PRIZE

Here is our highest goal, says Jesus, the one place in all creation where we can find treasure that is lasting—which is, *the life that is deeply satisfying and full of joy that does not end.*

> *Every worry is a sign that we are sliding backwards from the presence of the Lord, with whom there is always perfect peace.*

You know and I know that in God's presence, there is fullness of joy. Where there is fullness of joy, there's no commotion and there's no trouble. God doesn't have to worry about moth or rust or thieves breaking in. Heaven is at peace. Sorrow is not there. Pain is not there. It isn't a place of regret. It's a place of fulfillment and a place of satisfaction in God.

Some who have experienced heaven by way of revelation or through a near-death experience quite often will tell us what they saw when they went up there. Some say everything there was so bright and beautiful, while others say they saw loved ones who were sick here on earth now healed and praising God. They tell all kinds of stories, but primarily these accounts all confirm what the Bible tells us anyway: In heaven there is perfect peace and security.

Heaven—that place in God—is so protected that there is no trouble or threat of trouble. Therefore, anything you preserve—that is, anything you put towards heaven by way of effort or material substance—you will find a benefit and reward waiting for you when you fully enter there. At the same time, you have the joy of knowing your soul is experiencing the greatest security your soul can experience *right now*. We can begin to experience a deep joy now that is only going to become more joy later. For God knows how to take care of us. We can begin to enjoy this blessed peace starting today, if we will begin to let Him take care of both the "now" *and* the "later."

Now with all these promises of care and security, why then do we become so preoccupied with things that offer us no lasting peace or security? So enthralled with them, in fact, that we slack our walk with God, and sometimes even go away from Him?

You see, it is all too easy to backslide. To backslide means, simply, that you are sliding backward...away from the goal you were once pursuing. Many of us are sliding ever so slowly and don't even notice we're going backwards. A little lust of the eye here, a little pride of life there, a bit of covetousness.... All the while we're going backwards, slipping further from that place in God—but it's happening so gradually we do not perceive it. Given time, however, the erosion becomes evident.

You used to pray regularly, fervently. Then you let other things crowd out prayer, and now you are backsliding in your prayer walk...and you don't even know it.

You used to read the Word of God constantly. Every time you found a Bible, you just felt like feasting on its richness because you used to have devotion with the Word. But then you get occupied in TV or your golf game or *anything* else...and there comes a time where you don't even feel like opening the Bible.

You used to win souls. There was tremendous excitement for you in doing this. You won souls everywhere. But there came a time when it hardly mattered to you whether souls were won or not.

There was a time when you used to worship God. If the church doors were open you were there. Any time you worshiped God, you just felt like weeping. But now you don't remember the last time God touched your heart. Here is the question: Do you even remember when this backsliding began? What was the first step backward? and the next, and the next...? Few of us know it when we are starting to slack-off and beginning to backslide. But there are two major attitudes that will warn you when you are backsliding.

TWO WRONG ROADS

The first attitude that warns us we are backsliding is preoccupation.

Many of us become preoccupied with our job or career. We may think, "The success I gain here, or the level of income I make here, will give me my sense of purpose or importance." Or it may be that we've just fallen into a rut, and paying the bills has become our number-one preoccupation. Our focus is, "I have to get up at six o'clock to be at work at eight, so that means being in bed every night at ten." Just like a little caged animal on a treadmill, we are driven— in constant motion.

Or we may be preoccupied with another person, or raising our children, or a hobby.

We can even become preoccupied with "spiritual good works." I can tell you that I know many men and women—those in the ministry full-time, and those serving the Lord in churches—who are preoccupied with "doing the work of the Lord."

When we become preoccupied with life and earthly things—even "things of the Lord"—*and not occupied with the Lord himself,* we have begun to backslide.

The second attitude that will drag us backwards every time is *worry.* Worry is a kind of preoccupation, but it's a negative kind. And worry is a very powerful force. It's a negative preoccupation, based in fear, and focused on something we are afraid to lose.

Some of our worries may seem great in our eyes. We may worry about losing our job, our home, our health, or someone we love. Maybe we've lost a job, and we're worried about how to put food on the table and pay bills. Other worries are more petty, but they occupy a lot of space in our heads and hearts! We may worry about whether or not the house looks nice all the time, or if we look our best. We may be perfectionists, caught up in keeping every detail perfect.

God, the Heavenly Vine-Dresser, carefully prunes everything that keeps us from that place of joy in Him.

Whether your worries are major or minor, every worry is a sign that we are sliding backwards from the presence of the Lord, with whom there is always perfect peace.

When earthly preoccupations pull us out of our place in God, we always find ourselves on shaky ground, stressed-out and in fear. We need to hear the Word again—and to encounter Jesus right there on that shaky ground where we have wandered.

"Take courage!"

In Matthew's Gospel, we find a situation in which Peter was most definitely preoccupied—with a lot to worry about.

In Matthew 14, Jesus' disciples wanted to go out one evening on the Sea of Galilee to fish. They set out in a boat, but Jesus decides to stay on the shore. The men are not out long, however, before a storm blows up. The moon disappears behind clouds, the wind rises, and soon great waves are threatening to overturn their little fishing vessel.

Suddenly Jesus appeared, walking toward them on the water. Before, they were worried enough, with the storm menacing them. Now, at the sight of a man's form approaching on the waves they were all terrified, thinking *"It's a ghost!"* (v. 26).

The first thing Jesus did was to address their worry. And He did it by revealing himself to them. *"Take courage! It is I..."* (v. 27).

"Lord, if it's you," Peter replied, *"tell me to come to you on the water"* (v. 28). This was a great statement of faith. Peter was saying, "I know that any place where you are, Jesus, there is the peace and power of heaven. If it is you, nothing can harm me, no matter how stormy everything appears."

So the Lord said, *"Come."*

Peter stepped out of the boat and walked a few steps... right on top of the water! Talk about walking in miracles! Peter had found that place in God where the unimaginable and impossible occurs.

But then something happened. Instead of keeping his eyes on Jesus, Peter looked around. *"And when he saw the wind, he was afraid....*" At that very moment, Peter lost his place and began to slip down under the rough, dark water (v. 30). Jesus had to reach out His hand and drag Peter up to safety.

Peter was taking part in an amazing miracle. But then He took His eyes off Jesus and began to sink.

Perhaps you have never considered this particular incident in this light, but it is a perfect illustration of what it means to backslide. And it shows us that any one of us can lose our place in God, no matter what kind of great miracles or experiences in God we have had.

Peter had heard the Lord say, "Take courage." He was witnessing an amazing miracle. He even became part of that miracle. But then he took his eyes off Jesus, and allowed himself to become distracted and preoccupied with the wind and waves again—with everything he'd been worrying about before he'd stepped into his proper place in Christ.

What was his place in Christ? What is the proper place for every believer?

The Place of Abiding

The place to which God invites every one of us is the place of simple trust in Him.

"Simple?" you ask. "It is no 'simple' thing for me to trust in God."

Yes—trusting in God is simple. We are the ones who complicate our walk in faith by taking our eyes off of God and allowing our minds and hearts to slide back down from that place where we meet Him by revelation, back into the tangle of earthly things.

Simple trust is the way we stand firm in Christ. It is the way we dwell, or abide, in the peace of God. Psalm 91 gives us clear instructions: *"He who dwells [remains] in the secret place shall abide under the shadow of the Almighty"* (v. 10).

Peter could have walked all night with the Master if only he had remained focused.

Too many of us never find our way to this place of simple trust. And others let our thoughts and emotions control us, and let circumstances dictate where we will stand spiritually. So we feel as though we're standing firm in Christ, abiding in God, one day, but, often, that's the day when very little is challenging our faith. Then the next day, we are thrown out of the place of standing and abiding when darkness comes and the storm arises and our boat begins to rock even slightly.

We are like Peter. We walk by sight and not by faith. The Spirit of God, who makes our firm place in God, however, is not seen and followed by the human eye—only by the eye of the Spirit.

Consider what Jesus told us about the Spirit, in John's Gospel, when He told the disciples He would be returning to God and they would not be able to see Him physically any longer (14: 16-17): *"I will ask the Father, and he will give you another Counselor to be with you forever—the Spirit of truth. The world cannot see him, nor knows him. But you know him, for he lives with you, and will be in you."*

I am certain these disciples were feeling very preoccupied with worry. Jesus had just told them He was going away soon and they would not be seeing Him again. And so He was telling them how to find that place in Spirit where they could stand firm and calm, and where fear could be replaced by quiet and unshakable joy. He says,

"I will not leave you as orphans. I will come to you. Before long, the world will not see me anymore, but you will see me.... If anyone loves me, he will obey my teaching. My Father will love him, and we will come to him and make our home with him" (vv. 18, 23).

In this passage, Jesus tells us there is one way to remain in that place with God and not backslide. It is to keep ourselves from being preoccupied with the things of this life by keeping our eyes fixed on God. It is to abide in the Lord.

You see, abiding in God is primary, because if you do not abide in that place with Him the cares of life will make you sink in spirit down to the muddy bottom to be buried by earthly concerns and fleshly diversions. In this sea of life, if we do not abide by faith in the love of God, when problems surround us they will cover us like waves. Then our faith will be washed out by waves of fear—and we will lose our place and our peace.

PRUNING

Now learning how to abide in that place with God is not something that happens overnight. And it takes an operation of God to keep you there.

In John 15, Jesus likens this process to the work of a vine-dresser with his vines. He says,

"I am the true vine, and my Father is the gardener. He cuts off every branch in me that bears no fruit, while every branch that does bear fruit he trims clean so that it will be even more fruitful" (v. 1-2).

What is the work of God? It is to prune. The Heavenly Vine-Dresser carefully walks around you, His lovely vine, to see what parts of your life are spiritually unproductive. He looks for parts of your life that are weak or diseased. He looks for things that are weighing you down needlessly. He knows that every one of these things will keep you from the place of health and productivity and joy.

> *The joy of the Lord only comes in a Christian's life when he or she begins to bear fruit.*

And so God goes to work—pruning. He begins to remove those things that are not good for us.

Our response is usually—"No, Lord! That's just the thing I've been praying about, asking you to protect and keep. That branch is so dear to me. Do not take it from me. It will cut me too deep, and I won't be able to stand the sadness and pain of losing that."

The Lord says, "If you want to remain in me, it must go."

And what is our part in this process?

It is to say, "Yes, Lord. It's true that giving this up may hurt for a short time. But I am going to simply trust that you know what is best for me. You alone know how to make me live in perfect peace. I will submit to your pruning."

Our part, as Jesus puts it, is simply this: *"Remain in me, and I will remain in you"* (v. 4a).

Our part is to abide in God. To stand firm in Him, not only when outer circumstances try to pull us away from His presence.

But also when He works to remove the very things from our lives that are distractions. And when He takes away that which keeps us from bearing the spiritual fruit He longs for us to produce. For He knows it is the fruit of righteousness and joy that will feed us in spirit and give us the kind of life for which we long.

The joy of the Lord only comes in a Christian's life when he or she begins to bear fruit. When you don't bear fruit, you don't have joy. But when you see your life being productive, you have joy. You begin to say, "The good things of God are happening in my life now. Good is being done in and through me. I am doing what God has called me to do, and being who God has called me to be.

"Most important, I am abiding in the vine and the vine is in me. I draw my life from the vine. I am a branch. The life is the vine, and there's a husbandman who keeps making sure that the branch is supplied with all that is required to sustain its connection to the vine."

"RETURN TO YOUR FIRST LOVE!"

Have you become preoccupied—distracted or worried? Have you backslidden in your walk in God?

The Spirit is always saying, *"Return! Return to your first love! Remember the heights you have fallen from and the place in God you once knew!"* (see Revelation 2:4-5).

Begin each day in God, in prayer. Walk in God throughout the day, in praise. Take time out to abide in Him—in those odd moments through the day when duty and work are not demanding your all, and worship Him. Lay down at night, committing your soul to Him, to commune with Him even during the night hours. Let the fire of God keep on rekindling in your life, because God is calling us all into that place in Him. When you commit yourself to abide in the Lord, He will become more fully present, strengthening you, steadying you. Giving you peace and joy.

Remember Jesus' command—which is also a wonderful promise:

Abide in God. And He will abide in you.

Chapter Seven

"THERE"

"WHERE is God in my life?"

"I am so spiritually dry."

"I don't understand why God doesn't answer my prayers."

"I'm going through a dark time. Why has God left me?"

"I need to know my purpose—my mission in life."

At the outset, we went to the root of all our longings—to the one question from which all these others ultimately spring: "Where is God in my life?"

What we have learned is that, wherever our journey in spirit has led us, God has been with us all along the way. He is never passive; He is always active. He is invisibly present, and influencing every aspect of our lives each day. Like the Good Shepherd He is, the Lord leads us along the paths on which He wants us to walk in order to get us to that place in Him.

Had we known what lay ahead, many of us would not have chosen the paths in life we have walked. Some of us have been sitting comfortably in the pews, choosing rest, comfort, and ease—only to find it has deadened our spirits. Some of us have chosen wrong or difficult paths, and then had to make our way back to God. Others have thought we were doing all the right things, but did not find the rewards we were hoping for...only a hard path.

Then there are those who have been taken on life's most difficult or troubled paths, but now, in the Lord, they can say, "My life has not been easy, but I can see now that there was no other way I could have gained so much or come to know God so intimately. God knew exactly where I needed to be—and I'm glad He got me there."

Not long ago, an elderly saint, a man who had gone through much in his life, spoke about his life in God. He had served the Lord through every kind of up and down. Now there was a kind of glow, a kind of glory, about him. He had a prophetic ministry but, more than that, to speak with him was like hearing from the Lord. Many were listening eagerly to this man, hoping perhaps he would share some great spiritual secret of how he has arrived at such a great place in God. What he said challenged us all:

"In my many years in the Lord I have come to realize one thing," he said. "Most of us confuse the idea of coming to that place in God with the idea of 'arriving.' We want to arrive at some point where it's all done. Where there is no more to do. Nothing more to learn. No more directives from the Lord to obey.

"But the problem with wanting to 'arrive,' " he went on, his eyes sparkling, "is that then there is no more adventure in God. No more growth. No more transformation into His likeness. As Paul said, when we are walking in the Spirit our life is all about *'being changed from glory to glory'* (2 Corinthians 3:18). That is one of God's greatest gifts to us—*a place inside His glory.* For the Father wants to open wide His arms and take us into that secret and glorious place in Him. But most of us really don't want that. We just want Him to make life better for us here.

"When that's true," he continued, "we stop following after God and try to take over the lead. 'Come here, God' we say, 'and make this place bet-

> *Like the Good Shepherd He is, the Lord leads us along the paths on which He wants us to walk in order to get us to that place in Him.*

ter.' Meantime, the cloud of glory moves on, and we are left behind.

"What is most sad—perverse, really—is that then we blame God, or we wonder where He has gone. But His great command to us has never changed. When He said, 'Abide in me,' He didn't mean 'Let's settle down and not go anywhere.' He said then, and He still says today, 'Follow me.'

"And that," he concluded, "is because He still has work for us to do with Him as He prepares for His Father's coming kingdom."

"RISE AND WALK"

The truth is, most of us want to settle down right where we are, thank you very much. And we want God to help us prepare our kingdom. But as the Bible warns us, this world and all that is in it are passing away. God wants us to follow His Son, Jesus, our Lord, as He prepares an eternal kingdom—a place in God where we can live with Him forever and ever.

This was Jesus' primary intent when He spoke to His disciples about the way to follow Him. Most of us have only our own interests in mind as we go to prayer—but Jesus' interest was the Father's glory. This motive is behind everything He said when He taught us about being followers after God and about prayer.

> *The truth is, most of us want to settle down right where we are, thank you very much.*

Consider this, one of Jesus' central and most important teachings, on the subject:

*"I tell you the truth, anyone who has faith in me will do what I have been doing. He will do even greater things than these, because I am going to the Father. And I will do whatever you ask in my name, so that the Son may bring glory to the Father. You may ask me for anything in my name, **and I will do it.**"*

—John 14:12-14

Most of us are addicted to the part where Jesus says, *"Ask of me anything and I will do it."* We want to skip over what comes first and get right to the good part—that is, the part where we get what we want.

But in the first part of Jesus' statement He says, *"I tell you the truth...."* Jesus uses this phrase every time He wants us to know He means what He says, to drive home His point with great authority.

For Jesus wants us to focus on this fact: "*If you have faith in me, you will do whatever I have been doing*"—and not only that but "*greater works than these shall you do, because I am going to the Father...so that the Son may bring glory to the Father!*"

Now what are some of the things Jesus did when He was on earth? Most of us are amazed by the fact that he healed the sick, opened blind eyes, made the deaf to hear, and—most impressive of all—He raised the dead. What could be more miraculous, more awe-inspiring, than that? *But these were just a sampling!* The Apostle John makes the stunning statement that *"Jesus did many other things as well. If every one of them were written down, I suppose that even the whole world would not have room for the books that would be written"* (21:25).

John is actually saying to us, "What you know about the Lord— that He healed many, that He walked on water, that He saved lost souls, that He fed thousands miraculously—*these things are just an introduction to the mighty works of Jesus!*"

As great a miracle as it is, when Jesus calls any one of us to follow Him out of our spiritual deadness—saying, "Rise and walk!"— there are greater miracles He wants to do *through each one of us* as He prepares His Father's kingdom.

"WHATEVER YOU ASK..."

"*...anyone who has faith in me will do what I have been doing...Then whatever you ask the Father in my name, I will do it*" (v. 12, 14).

So many of us approach this scripture as if Jesus is giving us a magic formula. You see, every one of us still has needs in our lives.

Just because we came to Christ, it doesn't mean our lives are perfect, or at peace, or that we are free from want of some kind. We need food and clothing, money for the rent and for groceries. We need to be healed in spirit and body. We hope that Jesus is still saying, "Do you know all those needs you have?—just ask God in my name and—presto!—they will be taken care of like magic."

Because God cares for our every need we can stop making the small things of life our big focus.

But that is *not* what Jesus is saying. As we saw in an earlier chapter, Jesus has already told us how to deal with those needs. In His Sermon on the Mount He told us, in effect, "When it comes to your basic needs, just trust in the Father. He cares for you. In His timing and according to His master plan, He will take care of those things."

Jesus was telling us, "All *those* things are already in a special category. They are: *Things the Father Knows About and Will Take Care Of.*" So we can set them aside, as it were. So we can stop making the small things of life our big focus. You see, as long as we are focused on the little things of life, important as they are to our basic well-being, we are stuck right there. But once our hearts are at rest, knowing we are cared for by our loving Father, we are free to go on and do what Jesus is talking about here—that is, "greater things."

Now you would have to agree that, if you were to see "greater works" done in your life your faith would become stronger and bolder and you would grow more in the Lord. Isn't that right? But the reason why most of us are not growing more is because we stay stuck in the small things. We major in the minor matters of life. We don't get great answers to prayers because we do not pray and ask for great things. So how can we get fired-up for God? Even at our best, we are only lukewarm!

"Greater Works"

The "greater works" Jesus has in mind, when He tells us to ask anything in His name, are the works of God that will usher in His kingdom. After the Cross, and our redemption, that was Jesus' next greatest work.

You see, the Lord will bless those who bless Him first. When you and I are following Jesus, seeking to do the great works that will spread God's kingdom into the lives of others, then when we pray we are asking Him for something "in Jesus' name."

> *Because God cares for our every need we can stop making the small things of life our big focus.*

What are those greater works? The first great work is this: *Total and complete surrender to the will of God.*

And do you know what the last great work is? *Total and complete surrender to the will of God.*

In one way the believer's life in God is simple. We must surrender our will to Him, and let His will rule in our lives. When we are following Christ, abiding in that secret place in God, then no matter what happens to us outwardly God is honored and glorified through us. That is the greatest work of faith any of us can do. It is, at the same time, the most challenging work we can do.

As we near the close of this book, I want to exhort you: *Stay in the Lord.*

No matter what storms, no matter what difficulties you may encounter, stay in the Lord. No matter how wise or smart you are, stay in the Lord. No matter what direction in life looks good in your eyes, stay in the Lord.

The truth is, the moment we take our eyes off the Lord, like Peter on the stormy sea, we sink down and slide back. When we rely on our own smarts, we have failed in spirit. When we trust in our own eyes to lead us we follow after the things of this earth and are soon led astray.

> *We major in the minor things of life. We don't get great answers to prayer because we don't pray for great things.*

All the while we are on our journey in this life, you see, the devil is watching. Yes, he is waiting to devour you. But he is also waiting for an opportunity to dishonor and discredit God. He can dishonor God in the eyes of others who are watching us *if* he can tempt us to wander out from our place of strength and safety in God's will. The moment we step out on our own, satan says, "This is what I've been waiting for—for you to move out from your place of abiding in the Lord! You think you can go through this storm without relying on God? Try it! You'll sink and die. You think you can solve this problem with your own understanding? Go right ahead! You're sick...or you need to restore your family...or you need to find direction for your life? Why wait on God? Do it yourself!"

The devil loves people who believe they do not need the Lord. He especially loves believers who say they are trusting in God but who are *really* trusting in their own power and might. "You say you don't need the Lord?" he says. "Wonderful. Because you are going to lead other people away from God with you. And that's just what I want."

The truth is, we can step out of our place in God and for awhile we will usually advance. Things go all right for a time and we think, "See, I knew I could solve this problem." After all, you're an intelligent man or woman, right? Maybe you're even a real man or woman of God. In our self-deception we have wandered into the camp of the enemy. Satan is leading us right where he wants us to go. To destruction.

What is so sad is that many believers are not walking in total surrender to the will of God. Instead they are walking in *self-deception*. All the time they are praying—five minutes a day!—and thinking they've done God a favor. But in their heart of hearts they really believe they know how to fix every problem by themselves. They don't really want God intervening in their lives because they have secret parts of their lives they don't want Him to touch.

Do whatever you need to do to remain in the place of surrender to His will.

As a result of this condition, this half-heartedness, they start out in the Spirit but end up in the flesh. I tell you, in my years in the ministry I've seen men of God lose the anointing, and even lose their ministry, because they started in the Spirit and then ended in the flesh. I've seen women of God lose their families because they start in the Spirit and end up in the flesh. *Do not become one of these casualties!*

Instead, whatever you do, do everything to remain in that place in God. It is the place of surrender to His will. And in that place your soul remains strong and secure, no matter what happens.

"YOU ARE THE LIGHT OF THE WORLD."

In Matthew's Gospel, Jesus says of those who follow Him, "*You are the light of the world*" (5:14).

Now a light is a light all the time. Even in broadest daylight it shines. But when is a light most important? In the time of darkness, of course. When we stand in that place with God, no matter what is going on around us—whether our circumstances are "light" or "dark"—we live to the glory of God. When we praise and worship Him, we live to His glory. When we continue in Him in the darkness, we walk in His glory. When we serve with zeal, His glorious purposes shine in all that we do.

When we abide in that place in God, those in the world around us who are in darkness will see the light of His glory. Then, because of His light in us, they will come to Him and enter His kingdom.

I want to tell you about a Christian couple I know—a man and woman who found that place in God. They have been able to go through all things, anointed by His power and presence, and alight with the fire of His glory because they found that place in Him. They have been beacons of the glory of God through very dark times, and in a spiritually dark place.

Bishop Hartford Iloputaife was the youngest bishop in Lagos, Nigeria. He and his wife, Frances, were called to walk with God and serve Him in place of great civil unrest, danger, and violence. From very humble beginnings, Bishop Hartford and his wife learned early on to find that secret place in God and remain there. In 1989, when I was there, the church had grown to 3,500 souls. And as they served the Lord faithfully year after year, the church grew rapidly, beyond anyone's wildest expectations. Recently, they prepared to celebrate

their 10th anniversary their church num-
bered *15,000* strong! And Bishop
Hartford was not yet 40 years old.

> *What are those greater works? **Total and complete surrender to the will of God.***

As the church grew, God gave Bishop
Hartford a place of prominence in Lagos.
While other preachers were selling out to
all the corruption of that country, he stood
for holiness and righteousness. Without
question, he stood out as a beacon of the
Lord's glory in a very dark place.

One day, paid assassins burst into their
home. First they shot Frances, and then they shot Bishop Hartford.
Their light was too much for the darkness.

I want to tell you, Francis survived the murderous attack, even
though she was shot *60 times!* Sadly, though, Bishop Hartford was
killed.

Now you can imagine the grief that Francis experienced. She
had never been in love with any other man but her husband. If anyone had a reason to leave her place in God it was this badly wounded, grief-stricken young widow. The doctors fought to keep her
alive, and could not even remove some of the bullets that had lodged
in her body because to move them would have killed her. With all
that she had been through, she could have left the ministry…and,
after serving God so faithfully and seeing Him move so mightily,
another woman in her position might have left their place in God
altogether.

After all, when this tragedy occurred, where was God?

"HAVING DONE ALL...STAND!"

Instead of turning from God, Francis *stood firm in Him.*

In the months following her husband's brutal assassination, she slowly regained her health. Soon she was able to walk, and began ministering again. Perhaps because of Bishop Hartford's martyrdom—because that is what it was—the church did not stop growing. The growth exploded! Now the church is over 20,000 strong! From this one great church, they are opening new mission churches in other places. They have churches in Caracas, and churches in Trinidad. They have even opened a mission church in New York!

You see, in the midst of terrific hardship, with every reason to leave her place in God, Frances Iloputaife did the only thing she knew to do. *She stood her ground in God.*

During her recovery, in fact, she was able to address the nation of Lagos. With all the boldness and zeal of Christ, she addressed those shadowy figures in the government who had ordered the assassination—those darkened souls, hiding behind their powerful offices. She told them, "You thought you killed my husband. But he is living. He is standing with Christ in God right now. And the work God began through him goes on!"

In light of this amazing story, please let me ask you some important questions.

When things go wrong, when life is flat, you want to ask, "Where is God?" But God is there to care for your needs, even those that arise out of tragedy. We have His promise. So the real questions, then, are these:

Who told you life was going to be easy? Who told you that, when you go through shaking, the thing to do is to run away from God? And even to blame Him? Who told you that, when you've waited a little while for an answer or for direction from God, and it doesn't come fast, the best thing to do is go out and do things your way?

The Apostle Paul states that God has no "favorites." He shows no partiality. (see Romans 2:11) Therefore, if Jesus suffered, do you think God will not make you and I go through troubles and trials in this life? If He did not answer His own Son's prayer in Gethsemane— *"Take this cup of suffering away from me!"*—why do we think He is bound to answer all of our prayers?

You see, God is calling us to rule and reign with Christ when His kingdom finally comes. Paul also asks us how we can expect to reign with Him if we are not willing to suffer for the sake of the kingdom?

Dear Friend—unbeliever and believer alike—the most important thing you must learn to do in this life is how to stand firm in God. (see James 5:8.) No matter what happens, fix yourself in that place in Him where, though the whole earth around you be moved, in spirit you are not shaken or cast down.

IN GOD, ALL THE PROMISES ARE YEA! AND AMEN!

Regardless of what happens, learn to stand in God. Press in. Find that place behind the throne, where you can share intimacy with Him and allow Him to share with you what is on His heart for the world. No matter what He leads you to, or asks you to do, as you abide in Him, He will sustain you. You will even pass through death into glorious life.

Then will your feet be firmly planted on the Rock that is God himself (see Psalm 18:2). Then His glory will shine in you, for the whole world to see (see Matthew 5:14), and satan will be cast out and not be able to triumph over you (see Psalm 25:2).

I hope that what you have read here has brought you to a place where, with all your heart, you can fervently express a sincere desire to find and remain in that secret place in God. If this is so, then let us pray together:

> *Do whatever you need to do to remain in the place of surrender to His will.*

Lord, I want to be back where you are at all times. I want to follow wherever you lead, so I will not feel distant or separated from you. I want to dwell in your secret place.

Lord, I desire to know your heart, and know you. I desire Father to worship and serve you, and to place nothing and no one before you. I desire to do nothing more than I desire to do your will.

Whatever you tell me, I will do.

Wherever you send me, I will go.

Whomever you tell me to love, I will love.

God, to you and you alone, all my allegiance is due. You called me. Wherever I have been disobedient to you—in breaking your commandments, in disobeying your will—Father, forgive me! Lead me back into your pathways. Let me press in again, close behind you.

Lord, I want only to live in that place in you. I want, from now on, to let your light of glory shine from within me—so that those around me in this darkened world will see your light, and come to you, and give you praise and thanks for who you are. Do not stop working in me, Lord, until I am purged of my selfish ways, and walking only in your will.

*Lord, what I want most of all is to dwell in that secret place in you. The place called **there**....*

Amen!

Chapter Eight

CULTIVATING THE SPIRIT OF PRAYER

"Ask and ye shall receive. Seek and ye shall find."

—Matthew 7:7

IT is an incredible thing that Almighty God, Creator of all the universe, tells us to ask Him in prayer for anything. You will notice that the *instruction* comes with a *promise.* He who asks, gets! If there is a breakdown in the getting, where is the problem? I believe it is because we do not ask; or if we do ask, we ask *amiss.* Erroneous prayers result from ignorance of the principles of God's Word, which governs all requests that God will answer. God's very nature prevents Him from violating His principles regardless of how fervent our prayers may be. To ask God to give you someone else's spouse, for example, is to ask amiss. God cannot be expected to act in contradiction to His own commandment, *"You shall not covet your neighbor's house. You shall not covet your neighbor's wife, or his manservant or maidservant, his ox or donkey, or anything that belongs to your neighbor"* (Exodus 20:17). Yet God has promised not to withhold any good thing from us. We know that He has also said, *"If you then, though you are evil, know how to give good gifts to your children, how much more will your Father in heaven give the Holy Spirit to those who ask him!"* (Luke 11:13). Even with the evil that lurks in the hearts of every man and woman, there is still the capacity to give good things to their children. If parents who are evil know how to give good gifts to their children, wouldn't our Heavenly Father be even *more* inclined to give His children good gifts? After all, His love extends beyond the capacity of any mortal being. He would be insulted if we answered in any other way than yes. Our Father goes far beyond what our natural parents can do. God wants to give to all His children. He is a giving God! He gives to us from His best. The problem is that we often have a misconception of what is good for us, so we fail to recognize when we are being blessed with God's best.

Every one of us is considered His beloved child. He is telling us that our earthly parents will make sacrifices for us and give what they can. But God is the Supreme Father. All fatherhood proceeds from the Ultimate Father. All that fathers are is supremely illustrated in the Heavenly Father. And this Heavenly Father declares that it is His desire to give more to us.

WHATEVER GOD SAYS, HE WILL DO

"So shall My word be which goes forth from My mouth; it shall not return to Me empty, without accomplishing what I desire, and without succeeding in the matter for which I sent it."
—Isaiah 55:11

"God is not a man, that He should lie, nor a son of man, that He should repent; has He said, and will He not do it? Or has He spoken, and will He not make it good?"
—Numbers 23:19

Whatever God says, He will do. There is no question or doubt as to the veracity of God's words. Does He, like man, repent or change

His mind? Does He break the promise? Does He honor His Word? Is it possible for us to say that God can be trusted to keep His word?

There are promises that God has given you; and there are some things that God has said to you. Many of you feel like you have been asking but you have not been getting. So where is the problem? If God promises to give when we ask and we are not seeing the answer, then there must be a problem, but it is not with God. The problem is most certainly with us and our human perspective and limitations. We are too caught up in days and weeks and months, instead of being caught up with God. If you experientially know the acts of God and the characteristics of God, then you should be at peace to trust God for the timing and the nature of the answer. The Word tells us, *"But do not forget this one thing, dear friends: With the Lord a day is like a thousand years, and a thousand years are like a day"* (2 Peter 3:8).

We live in a time/space world; God does not. The answer was already on the way—it just didn't arrive according to your time schedule. The answer was probably sent on the very day that you asked, but as it passed from the throne of the Father into our time/space dimension, a lot could have happened. We need to adopt an eternity mindset as we grow to recognize that God operates with timing and seasons.

God is true. He says, if earthly parents know how to give good gifts, what about Him? He is saying look, I never lie! If you are waiting for God to break His promise, look elsewhere, because God never lies! He is a good and wonderful God who cares for you and is

> *Whenever God speaks, His word is followed by the power to perform the word.*

> *The glory of God needs to be revealed to this generation, and it is only manifested when Jesus is glorified.*

ready to meet you wherever you are standing.

His intention is that every single word coming out of His mouth will not fall to the ground or miss its mark. *"He watches over His word to perform it."* God never moves unless He has first spoken. And whenever God speaks, His word is followed by the power to perform the word. That means, no matter what looks impossible; no matter what systems of this world declare undone; no matter what man says; if God says it, it will come to pass!

THE ENEMY OF GOD'S WORD

The devil knows the power of the spoken word. Therefore the devil will try to keep you from the spoken word. He will fill your ears with "other stuff" so that you cannot hear the sweet words of God. He will distract you with the things of this world. He will deceive you and convince you that God is not speaking and that He does not care.

When you are trying to constantly meditate and fill your spirit with the Word of God, and then all of a sudden a tragedy happens or you fall back into sin, the devil comes to discourage and condemn you. Because you are susceptible in that weakened condition, the devil will abuse you. When a person begins to backslide, his attitude toward the Word weakens. That person grows cold and distant concerning the things of God. This is the work of the enemy—intended to separate you from God and to distract you from prayer, praise and worship to Almighty God.

The devil is quite aware of the power of the Word. He will keep you from your wife, if she's in the Word. He will keep you from your husband, if he's in the Word. He will keep you from your pastor, if you move out of the Word. The devil knows if you stay close to the Word, you will find the ground to resist him. Unless the Word of God is in you, you cannot resist the devil. When you submit to the Lord, it means you have yielded to His Word. When you submit to the Lord, you resist the devil, and he can't do anything but flee from you.

THE SPIRITUAL ART OF ASKING

"And whatever you ask in My name, that will I do, that the Father may be glorified in the Son."
—John 14:13

"The thief comes only to steal and kill and destroy; I came that they might have life, and might have it abundantly."
—John 10:10

Jesus also declared that He is the way, the truth, and the life. Now, since Jesus is the way, the truth, and the life we should not *stutter* when we ask. We should ask with boldness and with faith. In fact, it is spiritually illegal for a child of God, a believer, to doubt Jesus or the Word of God.

The glory of God needs to be revealed to this generation, and it is only manifested when Jesus is glorified. How is He glorified? When things are done in His Name. That means, if the whole world began to do things in the Name of Jesus, God would indeed be glorified; or God would be abundantly glorified, because, the Name of Jesus makes the heart of God glad! When Jesus' disciples accomplish His works, God is well pleased. He brings us into His fold—the beloved in whom He is well pleased!

HOW ARE YOU ASKING?

The questions are: Are you asking? How are you asking? What are you asking? Why are you asking? When do you ask? Where do you ask? Most of us have been asking God for wrong things in the wrong places. He says, *"Ask and it shall be given you"* (Luke 11:9).

Does it mean that if I as a believer am not receiving from God, something is wrong? I could say yes. I've always believed that whenever you see a distance between yourself and God, all you have to do is identify who moved.

If we have been instructed by the Word of God to ask, then God has unique and different ways in which to respond. *"And in that day you will ask Me no question. Truly, truly, I say to you, if you shall ask the Father for anything, He will give it to you in My name"* (John 16:23). Asking precedes receiving. The problem is that we worry more than we ask. We complain more than we ask. We try to work out our problems before we ask.

> *"But if any of you lacks wisdom, let him ask of God, who gives to all men generously and without reproach, and it will be given to him. But let him ask in faith without any doubting, for the one who doubts is like the surf of the sea driven and tossed by the wind."*
>
> —James 1:5,6

How does God give? Generously. How did Jesus give? Generously. God is ready to give a very generous answer to every question posed by His children. He delights to answer and His answers are generous because they come from a Father who has a large and generous heart.

> *The devil knows if you stay close to the Word, you will find the ground to resist him.*

"*Now to Him who is able to do exceeding abundantly beyond all that we could ask or think, according to the power that works within us*" (Ephesians 3:20). What is this power? It's the Word. If the Word is in you and you are entreating God, your prayer will come out of the Word that is in you. When you ask the Father using your own words, you always conclude with your own emotions and thoughts. But if you ask Him according to the Word of God, you will come in Jesus' Name.

We often go to God and complain; we tell Him all that is going wrong. As we speak our complaints in His Name, we bring shame into our attitudes and disgrace His Name. However, if we come with the Word, then we can have confidence in our prayers. According to the Word of the Lord, whatever I ask my Father in faith, I receive. I have confidence in what Jesus is saying. Therefore, if Jesus says it, I believe it's going to happen.

James makes it clear that if you don't do it the right way, you will not get the right answer. You have to ask, and you have to ask properly. Your attitude will determine whether you receive it or you don't. You say, "Lord, I love you, I love you," and yet it is clear that there are issues in your heart. God says "I won't hear you, because you are not coming in Truth." When you come to the Lord, you have to make sure you come with truth, because he searches for truth in the inward part. You start your prayers with where you are standing! If you're not saved then that's where you start. "Lord, be merciful to me a sinner."

Don't pretend. God desires to bring you to a place where you will have influence in His presence. If you submit to the Holy Spirit and His spiritual work in you, then you will be able to *cultivate the right and proper spirit of prayer* and you will have influence in the heavenly realms.

FOR WHAT ARE WE ASKING?

> *Whenever you ask something of God, you have to expect that you will get an answer.*

For so long we have been accustomed to praying for manna. We have interpreted "give us this day our daily bread" narrowly—regarding it as a request for provision to meet our material needs for food to preserve our physical well-being. If we want to find a place called *there*, we must lift our eyes from the need for manna to our need for the Bread of Life. When our spiritual hunger and thirst for God and the things of God become so acute that we begin to petition Him night and day, praying without ceasing and pressing into Him with our request for more of Him, His word will not fall to the ground, and He will respond. God has promised to reward those who diligently seek Him. He cannot lie. Not one word of His shall fall to the ground. Now, Jesus told us not to cast pearls before swine. How likely is it that He will usher into His presence those who neither desire nor appreciate spiritual gifts and therefore are not willing and joyous to pursue His presence? *The place called **there*** is reserved for those who pursue His presence with intensity similar to that with which the lover seeks the beloved—as recorded in the Song of Songs.

For too long we have not given much time and attention to seeking spiritual gifts and, more importantly, the Giver of life, and experiencing these words, *"For in Him we live and move and have our being"* (Acts 17:28). When we approach prayer in the desire to know Him, we will experience the light of His countenance and will exult minute to minute in "my Lord and my God."

In all these things we shall be more than conquerors if in praying we shall ask, seek, knock—believing, trusting and in faithfulness persisting until our prayers and supplications are answered. Then the joy that His presence imparts so sweetens our lives, that we reflect His sweetness and radiance. Then all who come near us are touched by the radiation of the Spirit of the true and living God indwelling us. Then we are able to go about doing our daily tasks—glorifying God as we execute His will in all our activities.

EXPECTATIONS IN PRAYER

As we have seen, one of the reasons we don't receive answers to our prayers is approaching God with the wrong attitude. God wants us to ask, because there are needs in our lives. Whenever you ask something of God, you have to *expect* that you will get an answer. As we fervently desire and ask of God—believing, trusting, persisting in faith—our hope becomes more firmly established as each prayer is answered. Whether it be a yea, a nay or wait, as it is with a friend, our relationship with God is forged through the frequency of the time we spend together. The intimacy of prayer—speaking to Him and listening to Him with open ears—develops through time. Open hearts warm with affection are willing to obey. Our minds become joyful in obedience, and our hands offer no hesitation to executing the will of the Master. As we delight ourselves in the Lord in this manner, He rewards us with the Light of His presence on a day of His appointing and by His sovereign will. It is never because we have perfunctorily performed the duty of prayer, or specified the date and time by which we were requesting to be in that place called *there*. It is not our prayers only, but our hearts and hands as well as our voices that we must bring as an offering. As we acknowledge our need for *Him*, more than necessary food, God will hear the heart cry of the believer. Hence when we arrive at the place where we cry out to Him for more of Him, we will become familiar with *a place called there*. His Word will not return void. This gives us the assurance that all who seek Him with all their hearts will find Him. Friends, if you covet that place, I ask you to join me in this prayer:

"Father, I want to be an intercessor. I want to have an intimate relationship with you, O Lord. I want to cultivate a spirit of prayer, in Jesus' Name. Change my attitude. Change my motive. Change my heart. Change my thinking. Change all those things, O God. I yield totally to You. For too long I've been pleasing people. For too long I've been trying to impress people, but yet, underneath in my heart, I know I need a touch from You, Lord. I give my life to you in the desire that I might become a person of prayer. Touch me and help me, Lord, to truly culti-vate a spirit of prayer. My heart's desire is to draw nigh unto you, Lord. Father, I want to know You! I pray that you will meet me in the secret place and that with your guidance, I may experience "A Place Called There." Lord, once I have learned how to get there with You, please help

me to go often and develop sweet communication and intimacy with You. I thank You, Lord, for answering me and I look forward to meeting you often. In Jesus' Name, I pray! Amen.

Epilogue

THE SHADOW OF A PRESENCE

*E*VERYTHING *in life has a shadow.* Whether an inanimate object or a living thing, all objects cast a shadow. Anything, whether dead or alive, has the potential of throwing a shadow. Simply speaking, a shadow is created when a certain object is positioned into the light. The object cannot create the shadow on its own. It is the union of the entity with the light that creates the shadow.

Jesus said, "*I am the light of the world,*" and when men or women stand in the *place* of that light, then their lives, in union with the Light, cast a powerful shadow on the earth. We have passionately explored that celebrated *place* of His presence and the compelling power that the presence of God has on a human life. We have seen that it is a place that we must seek after and pray for. Sometimes, it is a dark place where the light is obscured by the darkness of heartache and trouble. Without a doubt, it is a place of service and obedience and always, it is a place found in the heart of God. It is *a place called there.*

David, the sweet psalmist of Israel, made the dwelling *place* of God the primary pursuit of his life.

One thing I have asked from the Lord, that I shall seek: That I may dwell in the house of the Lord all the days of my life, to behold the beauty of the Lord, and to meditate in His temple.
—Psalm 27:4

David was not content with a weekly visit into the place of the presence; he wanted to "hang out" there all the time. In fact, he built a little tent in his back yard, called the tabernacle of David, where the ark was placed so that he could continually abide *there* in the presence of God's glory. How he loved that place!

O Lord, I love the habitation of Thy house, and the place where Thy glory dwells.
—Psalm 26:8

Once a man has discovered that place he will never be satisfied with the "places" of the earth. His heart will always be inclined towards the heavenly regions.

THE SHADOW OF YOUR PRESENCE

Those who dwell in the light of His presence will cast a peculiar shadow on the face of the earth. The Book of Acts tells us that the shadow of Peter had a miraculous healing effect upon those who felt the shadowy cloud pass over them, "*to such an extent that they even carried the sick out into the streets, and laid them on cots and pallets, so that when Peter came by at least his **shadow** might fall on any one of them*" (Acts 5:15).

The question we must ask ourselves is, What kind of shadow does my life cast upon others? The answer to that question is determined by the environment of our inner life.

The environment in which you live will determine the character of the shadow you cast.

Those who live in doubt and disobedience will throw a dark shadow over others, drawing them into their own circle of despair and restlessness. These dark shadows, rather than drawing people, will repel them. Those who live under the *shadow* of the Almighty will cast a convincing and compelling shadow over others as they draw them into the light of His *presence.*

CALLED TO BE WITH HIM AND THEN SENT OUT

Too many people have chosen to go forth with the gospel before they have sat at the feet of the Lord of the gospel. It is in His presence that our lives are empowered to effectively proclaim the gospel. You cannot explain the gospel until you have experienced the gospel. As one learns to make the presence of the Lord his place of *habitation* rather than *visitation,* the result will be obvious to all. The Scriptures say that Moses' face shone with the glory of God. This extended time in the presence of God created a certain heavenly manifestation of glory that was cast upon others.

> *As one learns to make the presence of the Lord his place of habitation rather than visitation, the result will be obvious to all.*

But this is not the end of the story. Eventually, one must come down from the place of heavenly encounters with the glory and live among men. When Moses descended the mountain, he encountered the rebellion of the people of Israel. When Jesus came down from the mountain, He met the disciples' lack of faith. We are tempted to hang out in the place called there, but it is important for every disciple of the kingdom to understand that he must be willing to leave that place so that he can go to the place where men need him and his message.

...AND HE SENT THEM OUT

And He appointed twelve...that they might be with Him, and that He might send them out to preach.

—Mark 3:14

Just as it is true that some go out too quickly, it is also true that some go out too slowly. Some would be content to hang out in that secret, quite place forever. It is so secure and peaceful there. But this was never the plan of the Master. It was always His desire that after we had been with Him, in the *place* of His appointing, that eventually we would be sent out.

The things that we have seen and heard in the secret place must be declared in the public place.

"*What I tell you in the darkness, speak in the light; and what you hear whispered in your ear, proclaim upon the housetops*" (Matthew 10:27). The words we hear whispered in our ears by our loving Lord must be sounded abroad in all the earth. The secrets He shares, the truths we learn, the things that we have seen are not for our private pleasure; they are for the world. If you hoard the treasure it will become like the ancient manna and begin to rot in your soul.

In the place of His presence, as we listen to His words, we are being transformed and enlightened all at the same time.

*The unfolding of Thy words gives light; It gives understanding
to the simple.*
—Psalm 119:130

The entrance of God's Word is not just to thrill us; He longs to make us wise in the things of the Spirit. The wisdom of this world is passing away, but the wisdom discovered in the secret place is a wisdom that must be spoken in the society in which we live. Men are crying out for direction and understanding. They are also drying up because there is so little of the precious Word of God in our days. God's people hold the key and must discover and faithfully proclaim God's Word to this generation.

Also, in the *place* of His presence, we behold the beauty of His face.

*One thing I have asked from the Lord, that I shall seek: That I
may dwell in the house of the Lord all the days of my life, to
behold the beauty of the Lord, and to meditate in His temple.*
—Psalm 27:4

Standing in the presence of God for long periods of time will create its own reflection upon us. As we dwell in the light of His presence, our own shadow will cast a distinct and peculiar shadow upon the lives of men.

*But we all, with unveiled face beholding as in a mirror the glory
of the Lord, are being transformed into the same image from
glory to glory, just as from the Lord, the Spirit.*
—2 Corinthians 3:18

The Greek word for beholding is *katoptrizo*, which literally means "to reflect as a mirror." So Paul is literally saying that as we behold the glory of God our very lives will become a living reflection of the glory. Our lives will cast a powerful shadow emanating from the place of His presence. But for it to cast a light it must get out of the secret place into the world.

Also, there is a sweet fragrance that is attached to those who have dwelt in the House of the Lord. When they begin to move among men, that fragrance will be an attracting force for drawing men and women to Christ.

> *For we are a fragrance of Christ to God among those who are being saved and among those who are perishing.*
> —2 Corinthians 2:15

As we sit in the place of His presence the aroma of Christ becomes our aroma. As we behold Him, we become like Him.

> *For God, who said, "Let light shall shine out of darkness," is the One who has shone in our hearts to give the light of the knowledge of the glory of God in the face of Christ.*
> —2 Corinthians 4:6

Give to whom? The light shining in our hearts is for the world. It shines best in the dark places of the world. It was never meant to remain exclusively in your private place with God or in the corporate place of the Church. The light is for the world. You should never minimize the power of the shadow cast by the light shining in your heart! It can have a persuasive and powerful influence on those around you.

As you have experienced the light of His glory in *a place called there*, then let your light so shine among men that they will also be drawn to that *place*.

CONTACT INFORMATION

To receive our free newsletter and a complete list
of available resources from Kingsley Fletcher Ministries,
please contact the ministry at:

P. O. Box 12017
Research Triangle Park, NC 27709-2017

(919) 382-1944

www.kfmlife.org